JULIE WALTERS IS AN ALIEN

My daughter Maisie drew this impression of New York before I left.

JULIE WALTERS IS AN ALIEN

A Voyage to Planet America

Julie Walters
and
Graham Stuart

Hodder & Stoughton

Copyright © Meridian Broadcasting Limited 1997
Photographs by Stephen Morley copyright © Meridian Broadcasting Limited 1997

The right of Julie Walters and Graham Stuart to be identified as the Authors of
the Work has been asserted by them in accordance with the Copyright,
Designs and Patents Act 1988.

First published in 1997 by Hodder & Stoughton
A division of Hodder Headline PLC

10 9 8 7 6 5 4 3 2 1

British Library Cataloguing in Publication Data

ISBN: 0 340 69620 6

Designed by Behram Kapadia
Typeset by Hewer Text Composition Services, Edinburgh
Printed and bound in Great Britain by MacKays of Chatham PLC

Hodder & Stoughton
A division of Hodder Headline PLC
338 Euston Road
London NW1 3BH

Contents

JULIE WALTERS
IS AN ALIEN

D for Drama

Introduction

*T*he problem with my employment history is that I started at the top and it's been downhill all the way since then. When I was fifteen and still at school I managed to find myself the perfect job and all other work I've done since then has been a bit of a disappointment. This dream job involved helping a friend of mine called Christine Saranczuk run a sweet shop in Smethwick every Sunday. The shop was called The Bon Bon, Smethwick always having been very continental in its outlook. And it's such a long time ago now that I've forgotten how two little fifteen-year-old girls ever managed to look after the place on their own. The owner always seemed quite happy and trusting about what we did. Which was, if the truth be told, a little selling but mostly eating packets of crisps and sucking on Raspberry Whoppers, if you'll pardon the expression. In between sampling the stock we used to spend hours using the phone in the shop calling every single person we knew. Once we had exhausted our list of friends we used to resort to random numbers and play tricks on them. I fancied myself then as Smethwick's Jeremy Beadle. 'Hello, I'm from the G.P.O. and we need to test your line.

Would you mind whistling into your phone?' We laughed so much sometimes it was hard to eat confectionery at the same time. Work in The Bon Bon wasn't as much a first job for me as a passport to heaven. Happy? As a kid in a sweet shop.

What fifteen-year-olds quickly learn about life is that really good things never last and soon I had to say bye-bye to The Bon Bon. It was the summer of 1966 and while England were busy winning the World Cup, I was signing on as a part-time member of the backroom staff of C & A's in Birmingham. I was about to discover that not every job would be quite as sweet as my first experience. For some inexplicable reason my job title was packer but in fact all I ever seemed to do was *un*pack clothes. Me and the rest of the unpackers were trapped for eight hours or so in a windowless caged compound, well away from the customers, concentrating on the main task in hand. Namely, trying to make the time pass as painlessly as we could. We even managed to have some fun despite the unpleasant surroundings. The strange thing about the job was that I had to work at C & A's under an assumed name. Apparently, there was already another Julie Walters on the staff and the management insisted that I take the name Julie Bishop to make things administratively easier for them, I suppose. I have no idea why they chose the surname Bishop but at the tender age of sixteen I didn't have the courage to ask. So for that summer of '66 I did my very first acting job playing the part of Julie Bishop. The reviews were not particularly good and Julie Walters-Bishop and C & A soon parted company.

I was then about to go into my sixth year at the Holly Lodge Grammar School for Girls in West Bromwich with four O Levels already under my belt. My mother had suggested nursing as a possible career for me and because I was at the teenage stage of only caring about the day ahead rather than my long term future I didn't bother to disagree with her choice. I applied to the Queen Elizabeth School of Nursing in Birmingham and was promptly accepted. By this time I had completely lost interest in school and my attendance was a long way from perfect. In fact I was away from my desk so much that the school decided to make my absence slightly more official. Mr Taylor, the Deputy Head, approached me on one of my rare appearances in school and told me that I wasn't required back the following term. I was being expelled. Worried about the effect of that bad news on my parents, I took what seemed the adult way out of the problem by explaining to my mother that I had taken the mature decision to leave school myself. I think some politicians call that sort of behaviour 'being economical with the truth'. I explained very convincingly to Mum that there was no need for me to stay on at school because I wanted to start nursing right away.

It was around the time of all of this that I finally admitted to myself something I think I had known for a long time. I didn't want to be a nurse for the rest of my life, or do any other conventional job for that matter. What I really wanted to be was an actress. The idea came from out of the blue because there was no history of acting in our family, but something in me clearly said that I would only be happy on stage. I can vividly remember the first time I told myself the truth about what I wanted. I was locked in the precious privacy of our bathroom with the steam from a hot bath filling the air around me. I looked at my face in the misted mirror and found myself saying out loud for the first time the fateful sentence, 'I want to be an actress.' As I mouthed those words I felt strangely fulfilled but at the same time sad because I doubted I could ever say them to my parents in a million years. Mum and Dad would have been a bit surprised to hear my ambition because up until then I had only been on stage twice. Once as a very small child, and then a few years later in a school production of *A Midsummer Night's Dream* playing Moth, a part I won more because of my classroom bad behaviour than precocious acting talent. The only theatre I had ever seen was at Smethwick Rep and all I remember of the plays I went to there was a lot of orange make-up and hairy legs. And that was just the usherettes.

The nursing course didn't start immediately so I had to take my first full-time job to fill in the gap. I couldn't afford to be particularly choosy at my young age so I was stuck with what was on offer. That turned out to be the post of clerk in the Midland Assurance office in Birmingham and it was there that I was to learn just how painful office work could be. The dullness and sterility of the job almost drove me crazy and I really felt as if I was doing time in prison rather than working for a living. Life on the Midland Assurance chain-gang was made a little more bearable by the presence of my cell-mate, sorry, work-mate, Sue, who had an accent so thick you could lay bricks with it. She was just fifteen and when she found out that I was a whole two years older than her and still very much single, she told me that she personally would slit her wrists if she wasn't engaged by my advanced age. I never did find out if she succeeded in getting a ring on her finger before she hit the senility of seventeen but my money is on H. Samuels and Sue having done business.

The only way Sue and I could make each Midland Assurance day feel less like a month of hard labour was by messing around as much as we could get away with. Our favourite activity was spotting funny names amongst the thousands of files which filled every corner of the dusty office. Well, we were just teenagers. Discovering fantastic names like Agnes Bottoms and my personal favourite of Cornelius Crack in a mound of manila files could reduce us both to tear-stained and shoulder-heaving hysterics. When we had nothing to laugh about, the job got to me terribly and, maybe I shouldn't be admitting this, but on particularly bad days I developed a special system to lighten my office workload. It involved taking bundles of letters about long lost files which tended to mount up on my desk and storing them in a safe but unconventional place until we could deal with them. Down the loo. I did not last as an employee of Midland Assurance for long.

My sentence at Midland Assurance was mercifully short and within months it was time for me to escape to become a nurse. I dutifully enrolled on the SRN course at the Queen Elizabeth with the best intentions, but quickly discovered that I was not very suited to the job. I was actually terrified of most medical procedures and that had nothing to do with being squeamish but more that I lacked confidence in what I was doing. As I well knew, I was no born nurse. On the plus side, I did get real pleasure from looking after the patients and I found myself getting so close to many of them that I'd often go round and kiss them all goodnight after late shift. The Sister would have been furious if she had caught me, but the patients didn't seem to mind. Becoming so involved with the lives of all these people was very important to me but it did make my inevitable experiences with death all the harder to handle. It was devastating to come back from my days off to find an empty bed where forty-eight hours ago there had been someone I had washed, fed, laughed and joked with for days, sometimes weeks, on end.

My first hands-on encounter with death came inconveniently, as death usually does, during a very busy lunch time. I was going round a ward with the soup while the rest of the nurses and Sister were back in the kitchen organising the main course. The first bed I arrived at was occupied by a tiny old lady who had been very poorly, and she seemed less than interested in my kind offer of some nice lentil broth. After several attempts to attract her attention it occurred to me that, rather than just being indifferent to the soup, this poor old lady might have taken a turn for the worst. The absolute worst. I began to panic and frantically tried to remember the ward procedure for incidents like this. The Sister had told us that any deaths had to be handled using the utmost discretion because there were so many old folk on this ward. No patient wanted to see what would come to all of them eventually acted out before their eyes like some distressing scene from *Dr Kildare*. So, as casually as possible, I grabbed an icy wrist to look for a pulse and began to babble incoherently into the lady's ear to convince the rest of the ward we were having a nice little chat. My initial diagnosis was spot on – there was definitely no pulse. It was then I had my master-stroke which, if it worked, would mean nobody on the ward would be put off their lunch, including the little lady I was dealing with. I nonchalantly brought the table with the soup over to her bed and then attempted to force the soup spoon into her stiffening little fist. It took a bit of wrestling but I managed to get the spoon into a realistic position. Unfortunately my struggles had forced her hand up level with her shoulder and it now looked like she was in the process of lobbing a spoonful of lentils at the lady in the opposite bed. I had to leave her like that because I knew that any more grappling between me and the old lady would arouse suspicions amongst her neighbours and there already had been a few funny looks. So I left her in mid-chuck, and made a point of saying very loudly so the whole ward could hear me, 'Now you eat that up, Mrs Belling' before speeding off on the rest of my round wearing a fixed grin. Everything went according to plan until I turned at the top of the ward to head down the opposite side. At that moment I casually sneaked a look over to poor Mrs Belling's bed where I saw to my horror that she had slumped forward with her face now in the broth, or at least hovering millimetres from it. She looked for all the world like she was searching for the proverbial soup fly and was still brandishing the spoon at the lady opposite. People were beginning to mutter quite loudly and things could not really have looked worse. This was my first brush with death!

Throughout my time at the Queen Elizabeth I felt that I was in a kind of uncomfortable and unfulfilled limbo, just waiting for I wasn't sure what. I knew in my heart that I would have to leave eventually but I still had no idea of the best way to get into the world I wanted. I looked under D for Drama in the telephone directory. There was just one listing, for the British Drama League, and they were very snooty and unhelpful when I gave them a call. Then my career luck took a turn for the better when my first proper boyfriend, David Thompson, went off to Manchester Poly to read sociology and told me about a drama course which was run there. I knew immediately that this was exactly the right thing for me to be doing so I wrote to Manchester and, to cut a long story short, got in. I was overjoyed, but the hospital was utterly outraged that I should even consider giving up nursing for the theatre and phoned my mother to convince her to stop me. My mum needed very little encouragement on that score. She was a pretty forbidding woman when she was angry, so I had to get my brothers to stand between me and her when I went home to say that I was definitely going to Manchester. She was horrified that I would consider giving up a secure and respectable career like nursing for a job which was not only less than respectable but also, horror of horrors, didn't have a pension. Not even the thought of a poverty-stricken old age could make me change my mind and I knew that the time was right to put bedpans well behind me. I had found and was about to follow my true vocation and a new self-confidence filled me. When I had my interview at Manchester Poly I was asked why I wanted to be an actress. My new confidence gave me the conviction to correct their misunderstanding of my position. 'No, I *am* an actress,' I told the interviewing board. 'If you don't choose to take me on, that is another matter, but I'm still an actress. That is what I am.'

The rest is history because I have acted ever since and I must say that I feel blessed. All those years ago I fantasised about what my perfect career should be and I have more or less achieved it successfully. I could not imagine myself doing any other job, except on those certain days when I have thought seriously about giving up the profession. Those days are the ones just before opening nights in the theatre. Then I am filled with a kind of fear which is so intense that it makes me genuinely consider going back to the Midland Assurance office. However, once I make it onto the stage I eventually get on with enjoying myself once again. Live theatre may be scary, but it has always been the part of my job which has made me feel most excited and fulfilled. I remember when I was doing *Educating Rita* on stage at the Piccadilly Theatre in the West End early in my career and I felt the real power and magic of stage acting for the first time. On a good night the audience were so captured by the play and the character that I sensed that they were almost breathing with me. It felt as if I could manipulate them however I wanted, almost as if playing a giant musical instrument. I don't think I ever got that feeling in the C & A packing room but I suppose I might have got close once or twice at The Bon Bon.

So, 'Actor' is what it says on my passport and other than before opening nights I have never thought about wanting to change that. Then one day a few months ago along came some very nice television people asking if I might like to work in America with them. I asked to see the script but was told that there wasn't one and in fact this was a job in which acting wasn't involved. No smell of greasepaint, no roar of the crowd? Count me out, darling. Then they explained that they wanted me to explore America in rather an unusual way. Their simple theory was that the only true way to learn about a country required a great deal more effort than just travelling through it as a tourist or television reporter. To really experience what life was like in a foreign place you had to roll up your sleeves and join the local workforce as a foreign national with legal work status. In short, you had to become an Alien. They wanted me to forget about being an actor for a while, climb into my flying saucer and set course for America where I was to land and make myself available for whatever jobs they could come up with. I liked the idea because I've always had a soft spot for Americans but never felt that I have really got to understand them. Maybe, I thought to myself, if I visited their society as an Alien, even for a short time, it would give me a more privileged glimpse into the American way. And who knows? There might be a New York sweet shop looking for a trained salesperson.

PART ONE

New York

1

Welcome to the Dream Team

At the Four Seasons Hotel

*N*ew York, New York. I'd always thought the place had been named after the beautiful English city which led me to wonder what the choice of another place name by the early settlers would have sounded like. New Macclesfield, New Macclesfield, so good they named it twice. I suppose it has a certain ring. Actually, the York bit of the name had nothing to do with the northern city but was a tribute to King Charles the Second's brother, the Duke of York, when the town, then called New Amsterdam and in the hands of the Dutch, was claimed for the Crown by Colonel Richard Nicolls and four warships in 1664. So the name New York has stuck but occasionally I still liked to fantasise about the daily turnover of billions of market dollars happening in the New Penge Stock Exchange.

I love New York, a phrase I've always felt could make a good slogan, and I have been to the city maybe nine or ten times in my life. It has never disappointed me and that's the best thing you can say about a partner in any kind of love affair. The passion started early for me because I grew up in the Fifties in a house where America was seen as the Promised Land. My mother came from that generation which believed in America completely and I must have been influenced by her and her stories of this great country flowing with milk, honey, *and* unlimited Coca-Cola. I do remember that we always seemed to be watching American television shows like *I Love Lucy* and *Wagon Train* which meant we knew more about the United States than any other country in the world, including perhaps our own. The images of the towering New York skyline dominated by the Empire State and the sight of the Statue of Liberty out in the Bay were fixed in my impressionable head long before I got the chance to see them for real. That experience of seeing those places for the first time was an extraordinary one for me. To be standing at the top of the Empire State looking up towards Central Park was amazing, yet at the same time it seemed as familiar as the view from our back bedroom. The only difference was that the Chrysler Building was now standing where Mr Tompkinson's garden shed should have been.

I still got excited coming to New York and always had a touch of the old butterflies as I passed under the steely gaze of the US Immigration Service people with their Ellis Island mentality. 'Give me your huddled masses and I'll make them fill in a huge number of forms and wait for hours in lengthy queues' seemed to be the modern version of arrival in the New World. A few years ago when I was doing promotion for *Personal Services* the publicity company organised a round-the-world trip for me to talk about the film. Anyway, I duly arrived in New York for the first part of the trip clutching just a single ticket because the publicity company had all the rest of my onward travel tickets and I proceeded to walk through Immigration without a care in the world. Then the man with the steely gaze asked where the rest of my ticket was and I immediately panicked, imagined I had just committed a series of terrible crimes, and prepared to face the full wrath of the American judicial system. American Immigration staff all seem to have such intense patriotism that they suspect every single visitor to their country will want to stay permanently. Unless you can prove you have somewhere to stay, enough money to survive your trip, and a ticket back to where you came from, you ain't welcome. I was in trouble because I was looking short in the homeward-bound department. Mr Granite Features asked me to follow him to a featureless office. My brain then progressively shut down like the computer in *2001 A Space Odyssey* and I found it impossible to remember the name of the company which had organised the trip. This really did not impress old Granite Features and when I told him that I was in fact an actress publicising a film about prostitution in which I played a Madam, it sort of went downhill from that point. It took a long time for me to find that company name and he made me suffer until I could prove my innocence and be a free woman again. I still bore the scars of that experience as I passed through Immigration but this time Mr Steely Gaze had been replaced by Mr Witty Banter and I got to chuckle my way into the country.

It was exactly 6 p.m. New York time, five hours behind London, as I stood on the roof of one of the giant car parks at the airport. The sun had set and the sky was a blaze of red and purple with yellow streaks. The chemicals in the New York atmosphere help to create the most incredible light shows overhead and I was getting my first eyeful. The temperature was just above freezing and the air felt a lot colder and more prickly than London. As the chill began to creep into my jet-lagged bones, I was glad to climb into the car that arrived. Then I was off on one of my favourite journeys in the whole world. I will

17

never forget the first time back in 1979 when I travelled into New York from the airport, came over the Queensboro Bridge and saw Manhattan stretched out before me like some glittering futuristic forest. It just about blew, as we used to say a long time ago, my mind. All my partly exploded brain could register was that the view looked exactly like the drawing on the box of a Max Factor perfume called, by a remarkable coincidence, Manhattan. The perfume, by the way, smelled exactly like fly spray. Now in 1997 I was following precisely the same route, hitting the slim finger of Manhattan in mid-town at 59th Street, and the first sight of that electric curtain of skyscrapers still made me shiver. It was like that moment in the cinema when they used to blow films up from normal size to widescreen for effect. Just breathtaking. Then suddenly the concrete canyons closed in around me and the spectacular wide shot became a tight close-up. The sidewalks glistened wet, people hurried past with their collars pushed up against the bitter wind funnelling down the avenues, and steam belched from holes in the roads. I had flown 3,000 miles to make a film and I had chosen the only city in the world which takes top billing over any actor. Was I crazy?

The journey to the hotel was the beginning and end of the sightseeing part of the trip to New York. I had not come here to spend days jostling for position in elevators with packs of Scandinavian tourists carrying enormous orange backpacks or dodging long lines of Japanese culture junkies in the Metropolitan Museum of Art. No, I was here to experience New York the *Nine to Five* way, although I had been warned that those times were purely symbolic and that I should expect to clock on earlier and knock off later in all the gainful employment I got myself involved in. It was probably a good idea to get a good night's sleep and, fortunately, the people who had organised this trip had chosen one of the very best hotels in town for me. The Four Seasons Hotel on East 57th Street between Park and Madison Avenue was a fifty-two floored, architecturally stunning, five-star palace of leisure. Perfect. Unfortunately, the Four Seasons had been chosen as the ideal place not for me to rest my weary head but the ideal place to begin work at six-thirty the next morning. It transpired that the only bed in the Four Seasons marked out for me actually had someone sleeping in it at that precise moment and my connection to it would only come when I got to make it the next day. My hotel for sleeping in came from a different page of the New York accommodation brochure.

The Four Seasons was opened in 1993 and has to be one of the best-looking hotels in the world. It was designed by the distinguished architect I. M. Pei, the man who masterminded the Louvre expansion in Paris, and it looked pretty spectacular to me as I approached it on 58th Street at the crack of dawn. The hotel was a pleasing honey colour and its slim, almost delicate, shape rose nearly 700 feet into the Manhattan morning sky. The large and imposing base gradually gave way in a series of steps, marked by what I can only describe as Christmas lanterns on each corner, to a slim limestone tower which floated above the hubbub of the streets. I was no student of architecture but I decided that unless I was very much mistaken the Four Seasons was a fine example of the Post-Modern contemporary style with some tasteful Twenties and Thirties Americana references. Put it this way, I would have found it hard to confuse it with the Smethwick Station Hotel. I was deeply impressed by what I saw and that was just arriving at the tradesman's entrance. The Four Seasons front door was actually round the corner in 57th Street but as an employee I had to arrive where the sun don't shine. To be strictly accurate the sun wasn't shining at the other entrance either because it was a pretty horrible morning, a few degrees above freezing and with that grey sky which seems to suck the colour out of a landscape. I found a simple white door which was the staff entrance and opening it I passed from a world where people waited on me hand and foot to an unfamiliar world where my own hands and my feet, along with all my other bits, would be doing the waiting.

The first job I had been allocated at the Four Seasons involved an elaborate costume change. I was presented with an outfit which reminded me of the time I played Dick Whittington in panto. 'Julie Walters as Dick gives an immense performance of tightly controlled emotion,' *The Times* had said. Actually, I made that bit up. This costume consisted of a black overcoat and trousers with a matching cape, gloves and top hat. Remember what the Beatles were wearing in the snow scenes in the film *Help!*? Well, that is what I had to don to look the part as a hotel doorperson which was to be my first hotel post. I was also advised to put on anything I could find which would fit underneath my outfit without turning me into the Incredible Hulk because I was about to begin an eight-hour shift standing on the sidewalk in sub-zero temperatures. I was detailed to work on the rear entrance of the Four Seasons at 58th Street because the door there saw much more action than the more prestigious but frequently placid front entrance. Apparently, famous people preferred to use the less ostentatious 58th Street door and there was often a trickle, sometimes a torrent, of A-List celebrities pouring out onto the sidewalk there. I pulled down my generous-fit top hat (I didn't know how they sized them but I had definitely picked up an XXL) and prepared to venture out into the cold.

It was 7 a.m. and the temperature was reading one solitary, ineffectual degree above freezing. As I stepped out of the climate-controlled warmth of the hotel into the Manhattan chill, I noticed that there was a heating element glowing red on the edge of the canopy above the 58th Street door. Sadly, it was at least twenty feet above my top-hatted head and I could feel absolutely no difference to the bitter cold I was experiencing. Still, it's the thought that counts. I introduced myself to the two official Four Seasons doormen who would share part of my shift and they had the good grace to look as if they were freezing too. Mike McLoughlin was obviously the senior man of the pair and I instantly made a special career-enhancing effort to get on the right side of him. He had been standing outside the door of the Four Seasons since the day it opened back in 1993 and there was no doubt that all around us was *his* territory. Mike stood well over six feet, with the dignified bearing of a man the locals liked to call the Mayor of 58th Street but had the plump and rosy face of a cheeky leprechaun. When he smiled to greet me he looked almost cherubic and could not have been nicer but I could sense a toughness about the man which was more Bronx than Ballykissangel, if you know what I mean. His partner for this shift was Randy, which I thought was a surprise considering how incredibly cold it was. That witty observation went down as well with my new colleagues as a screening of *Personal Services* would have done at my old convent school. Randy Aiello was a short, dark man in his early forties with a face made up mainly of moustache, who had started out in the hotel business as a bell boy and worked his way up to being a doorman. Randy was happy to help a new recruit to the world of doormanning and quickly provided me with a selection of advice and a crucial piece of doorman technology which I had

21

not thought to bring. How was I to know that I might have to write things down?

I surveyed my new domain, or what little I could see of it from under the brim of my topper, and was not particularly impressed. A usual mid-town Manhattan cross-street with a never-ending stream of traffic, wide sidewalks filled with heavily padded New Yorkers, and a selection of jewellers and galleries on the other side. There was certainly a regular flow of people in and out of the hotel door but two doormen, three counting me, seemed a little over the top for the workload. How many people do you need to say 'Good morning, Mr Whoever-it-was-that-had-just-passed-by'? Within minutes I was making a hasty reappraisal of my reading of the situation. It turned out that working as a doorman was one of the busiest and most exhausting jobs I had ever signed up for in my whole life. The action never stopped and I was soon working so hard that people were warming their hands by standing near to me rather than to the heating element on the canopy. I had to be a one-woman luggage-carrying, people-directing, advice-giving, traffic-controlling, star-schmooz-ing, message-taking dynamo and this was not even a busy day, according to the boys. The doormen actually ran the relatively small area of sidewalk and street outside the hotel and as Mike liked to whisper in my ear meaningfully, 'If it ain't moving, we ain't making any money.' If the traffic moved smoothly, then the cabs and limos could get to near the door to pick up and put down residents, all of whom liked to show their appreciation of our traditional hospitality by forcing dollar bills into our frozen fingers. Americans like good service and expect to tip for the privilege, so extracting crumpled dollar bills from tired business-men became my mission. I was soon to learn a very important lesson about customer relations though. An expensively casual young man in a long leather coat, who was probably on his way to some state of the art recording studio, ventured out of the hotel and asked me to get him a cab. As I hailed one for him with a commanding blast of my official-issue whistle I noticed that he was fumbling with his wallet. When Mr Leather-coat-rock-'n'-roll-person then asked me if I had change of a fifty-dollar bill, he seemed genuinely upset when I told him that I didn't carry that kind of cash. 'You're a sweetie,' he said, '. . . I'll catch you later.' I felt the gentle glow of accolade spread down from the brim of my top hat only to have the feeling shattered when Mike McLoughlin called me over. 'Let me ask you a question,' he said in the flat tone of Queens. 'Do you really think all he had was a fifty-dollar bill?' The realisation hit me like a sledgehammer. That awful man had taken advantage of my good nature, some might call it stupidity, to avoid paying a tip. I'd been conned. At that moment a little bit of steel entered my soul and my transformation from Midlands girl to Manhattan broad was underway. It was time to kick bottom.

I was learning another big fact about New York. If you were to lay all the limos in Manhattan from end to end nobody would be in the slightest bit surprised. In fact, someone seemed to have done just that very thing in 58th Street right in front of my eyes. From the first moment I had stepped out onto the sidewalk, the street beyond had been dominated by a shiny black luxury caterpillar which crawled reluctantly past the hotel. Mike had told me how to recognise the different companies that sent these tinted monsters to pick up guests and I noticed that he stopped to have intense discussions with certain drivers. Interesting. I was told to keep the line moving and so I had to make regular visits to plead with drivers to go round the block instead of standing in line at the kerb. The rule seemed to be that if someone was important enough to be picked up by limo, then they had earned the right to keep it waiting as long as they liked. Try that technique with the number 43 bus, madam, and see how successful you are. Mike gave me a fright by asking me to drive one of the limos which had been left pilotless at the side of the road. It must have been thirty feet long – like an elaborate hearse, for people with a pulse. Mike advised me to take off my top hat and put it upside down on the roof so that if the driver returned and saw his precious vehicle moving he would know it was one of us doorpeople doing it. Otherwise, I realised a bit later, he might panic and take out a gun so that he could attempt to do a slightly more radical form of an emergency stop. I sank into the expensive comfort which a herd of Jerseys had popped their clogs for and tried to find a driving control with which I was familiar. I could certainly have adjusted the bass response on the Barbra Streisand track playing on the car CD player but I was finding it hard to identify the buttons that made the car move forward and then stop again. Mike pointed out that having my feet four feet from the pedals was not a good control idea so he showed me a little electric button to push which made the seat glide forward. I got the hang of the limo after that and as I glided gently forwards I felt like the captain of the *QE2* steaming out of Southampton Harbour.

The street had to be kept moving because Mike said so. Mike said so because the NYPD told him to keep the street moving. He had warned me that 'stroking' the police was an important part of my job specification. So I should be as polite as possible so that they would leave us alone and bother everyone else in the area. As it got later in the morning a line of delivery trucks joined the limo trail out in 58th Street and the traffic began to clot. Cue the police and right on time a blue and white car pulled up at the

Four Seasons door. My jaw dropped. Getting out were two policemen who looked as if they had been dressed by Jean Paul Gaultier – an S&M dream in black leather, silver buckles, and wraparound shades. Their sexy leather jackets were positively dripping with badges and weaponry, and one of them had the cutest little leather hat I had seen outside Old Compton Street. The officer without the hat told me rather brusquely to make sure I kept our street moving. We made suitable moves and noises to convince our butch friends that we were doing our jobs and the stylish law enforcement duo climbed back into their car and headed off, probably to do a little shopping.

The revolving door between the hotel and the street whirled all morning, dispensing well-to-do residents looking for cabs. I worked the short distance from door to cab with Mike's cardinal doorman rule ringing in my ears. His theory was that 70 per cent of the job was about schmoozing people and the better you could do it, the more you would earn on tips. The secret seemed to be knowing as many names of residents, staff, limo drivers and even cabbies as possible and to continually engage them in brief but focused witty banter. It seemed simple and it certainly worked. As the hours passed I ignored the cold which snaked up my legs from the icy sidewalk and concentrated on joshing with drivers, touching my forelock to residents, and smiling at everyone. Soon I was carrying a fistful of dollars and loving every second of the job. By that time I had been joined on the door by another bona fide doorman in the tall and bulky shape of Christopher, a deeply sincere and spiritual man in his early thirties. I may have loved the job but I was still nowhere near the state of fulfilment achieved by Chris who brought his intense Christianity to working the door. He was the kind of man who said to people, 'God bless you,' with the kind of conviction that suggested it was official. Chris brought more of a tangible warmth to the doorway than a thousand electric elements up above us could ever have managed. He even had a habit of bursting spontaneously into song and as his rich baritone echoed down 58th Street doing 'New York, New York' I decided that he was almost too good to be true.

What I discovered was that niceness pays. Extremely well. A bearded and rather scruffy-looking man in his fifties appeared out of the hotel and I thought nothing of it as Chris greeted him affectionately and helped the man put his case in the back of a large limo. After the man had gone Chris asked me to guess how much he had been tipped by him. Considering I was mainly picking up single dollars for my great schmoozing qualities I started to guess around the $10 mark for a regular visitor. I was not even close. Chris revealed that he had just been handed a staggering $150 for his brief burst of charm. Nice work if you can get it.

I had realised that the Four Seasons was rather more than just another New York hotel from the minute I arrived there but my time on the door absolutely confirmed its unique status. A special hotel attracts special guests and I was getting the opportunity to meet them face to face. Mike and Chris seemed oblivious to the wealth and eccentricity on display, even when the unusual Mr Meyer showed up. A phone call informed us that Mr Meyer was on his way to the door. Going inside the hotel to meet him in the lobby, I was introduced to a wild-eyed but immaculately dressed man wearing vivid blue suede shoes. He was obviously known to my partners who after greeting him bizarrely stood on either side of him and lifted him off the ground. I was invited to help and together we carried him out of the hotel and into a waiting limo. When I asked Chris to explain what had happened, he told me that Mr Meyer did not care to dirty his well-shod feet on the New York sidewalks so always needed to be carried to and from his car. Neither Mike nor Chris seemed to think that qualified as strange behaviour, or if they did, they weren't saying. In their world, if you could afford to be a hotel resident you had earned the right to do anything you cared to.

Fame also bought the right to behave individually and the Four Seasons was usually stuffed with stars, most of whom, my colleagues kept telling me, used the 58th Street door as their private entrance and exit. I didn't see any evidence until I found myself opening yet another limo door and watched as Tom Arnold, former husband of Roseanne, sauntered past with his family into the hotel. But much more exciting than that, later in the day I was to come face to face with a celebrity who, with a single perfectly teethed and tanned look, would turn me straight back into a sweaty-palmed teenager. The boys had told me that a certain Mr George Clooney, hunky star of *ER* and the new *Batman* movie, was dining in the restaurant and had a limo standing by outside our door. After several cold and disappointing hours, I had given up preparing myself to be of service to George in any way he required when the man himself appeared suddenly at the door and strolled over to his car. Although I was several yards away as he strode across the sidewalk, a sudden burst of superhuman powers meant that before he could blink his gorgeous eyes I was by his side and leading him to the limo.

Everything was going perfectly until, out of nowhere, appeared a strangely dressed, grinning gentleman with a ghetto blaster hanging round his neck and in an instant he was also walking with me and George Clooney to his car. What is the expression about a relationship being crowded if there are any more than two participants? What was especially annoying to me was the fact that Mr Clooney was locked in a deep conversation with this character, who went by the name of RadioMan, and was not paying me a blind bit of notice. RadioMan was one of those special kind of fans who get a category all to themselves. The category is 'nutter' and he could have been the President of it. The radio which gave him his name had apparently been presented to him by Whoopi Goldberg and he seemed to have an encyclopedic knowledge of the whereabouts of every major movie star currently in New York. George Clooney appeared to know RadioMan well and they had a lengthy and rather odd conversation which completely excluded me. The three of us got to his car where Clooney finished off the conversation with RadioMan and reached for the door. I immediately forgot my Four Seasons trained diplomacy, bundled RadioMan out of the way and grabbed the door of the gleaming limo. The flourish of my gesture was somewhat curtailed by a lamp-post right next to the car which stopped the door opening more than about eighteen inches. I'm sure it was only a small scratch I caused on the paintwork. George could not have been more under-standing and with a shake of his svelte hips he slid his perfect proportions through the gap onto the leather seat. I got a good look at him at that moment and saw that his face was bronzed to suncream-commercial perfection and looked so flawless it was almost unsettling. I suppose it was a hormonal thing but as I closed the door obscuring his chiselled image, I found myself bellowing, 'Love your bedside manner, Mr Clooney. . . .' There was no audible response.

Still weak at the knees, I needed to lie down on the pavement and took the opportunity to work through a couple of scenarios in my mind. One, that George Clooney had seen me as he got into the car, heard my voice, and been so entranced that he found himself unable to say anything before he was driven away. Or Two, that George Clooney still did not even know that I existed. I did not have much chance to work out the odds on either possibility before I got myself involved in a real and much less pleasant doorman incident which had started to develop out on the street. For the last few hours the traffic had been running smoothly in 58th Street as I and my colleagues caressed and cajoled drivers to keep moving and avoid causing a jam. Now there was a giant green oil tanker stopped right outside the hotel and waves of unhappy New York traffic were crashing up behind it. I took my courage in both hands and marched out to sort it. American trucks are so much more beautiful than the terrible ones we have in Britain and the offending vehicle was a stunning green Mack tanker with yellow piping and more chrome and lights than you could see in an average fairground. The driver was a youngish guy wearing a baseball cap and carrying a heavy-duty attitude. His view of the situation was that he needed to pump his oil and he was not prepared to move to allow other vehicles to pass because he would lose a lot of valuable time. My view was that a cheery smile and some healthy logic would change his mind. Apparently this driver was not a fan of logic or even good client/customer relations and only agreed to budge once my larger doorman colleagues gathered round his cab and supplemented my arguments. So it was not all sweetness and light out there on 58th Street. But apart from that incident I loved being a doorman. I suppose the novelty would wear off after a few years, but I finished that day feeling safe in the knowledge that if I ever had a shaky year in my acting career I definitely had another string to my bow.

It was time now, though, to try my hand at another kind of job which helped to make the Four Seasons run as smoothly as it obviously did. The next day I was to be a member of the housekeeping team or, to put it in English, a chambermaid. The team, which reputedly contained a chamberman, met every day for an early morning meeting run by the head of housekeeping, Karen Daid. As I took my seat wearing the smart uniform of black dress with white collar, I was in the old *Hill Street Blues* briefing which always ended with the words, 'Let's be careful out there . . .' Karen welcomed me to the cleaning force and briefed all of us about the correct angle of showerheads and a new approach to the distribution of towels in the bathrooms. She spoke with the quiet authority of a woman who was both ambitious and good at her job. I got the sense that if I did set a showerhead at the wrong angle I would have to explain the reason to her. The meeting broke up and Karen didn't actually say, 'Let's be hygienic out there,' but she was definitely thinking it.

My partner for the day was Audrey Barratt, a tall Jamaican girl who was a three-year veteran of the job. There were 370 rooms in the Four Seasons and each of the chambermaids was expected to clean around ten of them daily. I was being sent with Audrey to restore one of the larger rooms to its usual glory. We knocked and shouted our arrival at the room because the most common problem for chambermaids is interrupting a nude guest. No such luck on this occasion, however. Worse, the missing guests had decided to set me a real challenge because the place was a complete shambles. I found it hard to believe that we could make it pristine in the thirty-eight minutes' average time allowed per room. Audrey warned me that there could be no short cuts and that we were to be completely meticulous in every detail. To illustrate her point she told me a story about a fortunately unused condom left behind the headboards of a bed in one of the hotel's rooms which had not been spotted by the chambermaid. The next day a new guest checked in, followed a day later by his wife who then happened to find the rogue condom. Apparently, none of his excuses, including the truth, worked and he left the hotel with a limp. I found the whole idea of access to people's, especially famous people's, lives fascinating but Audrey was horrified at my nosiness. She had got the chance in her time to make up the bed of the likes of Michael Jackson but she obstinately refused to divulge any secrets to me of what she had found there. She preferred to save her breath for shouting at me as we attempted to make up the bed together. As a fully trained and experienced nurse I have always been proud of my mitred corners. The years rolled back to the Queen Elizabeth Hospital in Birmingham as I tucked the sheet under the mattress but Audrey was less than impressed. It had to be the Four Seasons way or not at all.

Once we had restored some semblance of order to the bedroom I took the chance to enjoy the stunning views from this room. We were on the thirty-second floor and looking south down Manhattan towards the Empire State Building; in the distance were the twin spires of the World Trade Center. A view like that was worth a million dollars although the hotel price was slightly cheaper. Well, not much actually. Audrey and I had to tear ourselves away from the widescreen perspective of New York to brave the bathroom where a single towel out of alignment could be a sacking offence. Impulsively, ignoring the consequences in the marbled splendour of the bathroom, I reached for a perfume bottle to give myself a soothing spray. Audrey almost had a heart attack as she warned me that the guest might smell the perfume on me and have me fired instantly. Tidying the bathroom was like taking part in some elaborate ritual where every tiny action appeared to have some hidden meaning. Towels had to be precisely one and a half inches apart with the pattern on them perfectly aligned, the end of the toilet roll had to be folded into a perfect V shape, and the bath soap had to be carved into a bust of President Clinton. I realised as I jiggled a towel a few millimetres to put it precisely in the right position that this job was not for me. I said as much to Audrey who was far too polite to jump for joy and shout her total agreement with me but I could see in her eyes that that was exactly how she felt. The truth was that I was not enough of a perfectionist and probably too much of a Nosy Parker to ever qualify as a Four Seasons chambermaid.

So, it was back to the hotel drawing board for another job I could do. My next assignment was a spell in the room service department. Now I have been a great fan of room service for many years but always as a customer rather than as a distributor so this was definitely going to be a bit of a challenge. My uniform for the job was a rather fetching white tuxedo with a black bow tie which I donned before heading down to the immaculate Four Seasons kitchens to learn how to position my chervil. Chervil is that strange piece of foliage which no room service butter pat is complete without, and in order to be a room servicer I would have to learn how to handle it properly. My mentor in the room service nerve centre was Felix, a smartly suited gentleman whose considerable shape implied that he might be an authority on all aspects of the room service menu. He was a man of few words and seemed to be under enormous pressure as the orders piled up for breakfast. It left me to do a fair bit of improvising as I prepared my first tray. I had a wave of my old cutlery dyslexia as I put the cutlery and napkins down on the pristine white of the tablecloth. Felix found the time to rush over and move them around to the correct positions and to tut-tut as he noticed a clear thumbprint in the butter next to the chervil. I had to confess that there had been problems for me getting the greenery to look good and I might have inadvertently brushed the butter with my thumb. Felix pointed out that the depth of the fingerprint implied that I had not so much brushed as attacked the butter. Eventually I managed to complete the breakfast order to the best of my ability and was close to the lift when Felix explained that guests usually like to have some kind of beverage to enjoy with their meal. I had made the tiny error of forgetting the coffee. Felix pointed out that he would expect his people to do literally hundreds of these orders in a single shift and every one of them would be correct. I caught the drift of what he was saying and prepared to make another career move.

Felix's obvious disappointment with me meant I was surprised and delighted to hear that he wanted to give me another chance. He had just received a large snack order for one of the most expensive suites in the entire hotel. The Ambassador Suite was on the fifty-first floor of the hotel and cost a staggering $4,000 a night. Only the Presidential Suite at $7,000 was more expensive and, interestingly, could never be used by the President because all the extraordinary security measures required for the top man could not for some reason be implemented in the Four Seasons. In fact, when the President was in town he liked to stay at the Waldorf. Anyway, it wasn't the President I would be serving but I guessed it would certainly be someone rich and famous to be able to afford the rates in the Ambassador Suite. The order was certainly not haute cuisine but it was complex enough for me. Spaghetti and meatballs, a burger with American cheese and fries, ice cream, Cokes, and not forgetting the chervil on the compulsory butter portions. It took me a good thirty minutes of running around the kitchen to get all the elements together but at last I was ready and Felix himself gave me the green light to take the heavily laden trolley on the service lift fifty-one floors up to the suite. I felt quite nervous as I arrived in the beige luxury of the Grand Suite Floor and knocked on the Ambassador door with a trembling hand. There was just time to straighten the napkins and bend the straws for the last time and then I was standing in front of a stunning Manhattan panorama shining through enormous floor-to-ceiling windows. I stood for a second clutching my trolley to find my bearings, then turned to discover who my distinguished guests were. Sitting at a table were two very small boys with hungry expressions. There was no sign of an adult presence in the suite so it appeared that I had performed my room service hard labour for the sake of the hotel's more junior clientele. Well, one thing was for sure, at least small boys would be easily pleased. I whipped the metal lids off the main courses and invited the boys to enjoy their meal. The elder of the two boys, his face beaming with the innocence of youth, looked up and said, sweetly, 'This is Swiss cheese. I ordered American cheese.'

I had seen a sign up on the wall of the staff entrance to the hotel. It said simply, 'Welcome to the Dream Team.' It is hard being British sometimes because our innate sense of cynicism can't really appreciate idealism when it is thrust in our European faces. The difference between our nations was summed up by the fact that there had not been a single piece of graffiti added to the sign. The Americans take an amazing pride in what they do and the staff of the Four Seasons, no matter how menial or lowly paid, seemed happy to believe that they were all official members of the Dream Team and lucky to enjoy the privilege. Working with Americans for a brief time had taught a cynical old Brit like me that we had a lot to learn from the New World. I had played for the Dream Team for only a few days so I suppose I qualified as their Short Stop! That, I have to inform you, is a genuine American baseball joke which you should look up if you don't find hilarious. Anyway, I found myself tapping into that sense of pride amongst the staff and enjoyed the whole experience. If I could take anything home from America, other than a case full of Buzz Lightyear toys, it would be their national attitude to customer satisfaction which makes the British, permanently class-ridden, often bitter, sometimes downright rude approach look like something from the Dark Ages, which it probably is. The reality is that Americans like to help people, enjoy being in teams, and absolutely love wearing uniforms. It's really no wonder that they invented fast-food restaurants.

A couple of days after serving my time on the Four Seasons Dream Team I had the bizarre experience of being invited back to have dinner in the hotel's plush Fifty Seven Fifty Seven Restaurant. As my cab pulled up at the 57th Street entrance I was so anxious to thank the doorman and make him feel special that I had virtually asked him to marry me by the time he helped me out of the taxi. Then we swept into the main entrance of the hotel and for the first time I appreciated what an amazing place the Four Seasons was. The foyer was enormous and its scale, combined with the limestone and marble interior, made it look almost cathedral-like. I felt naked walking through the place without wearing some kind of uniform but as I sat down to enjoy cocktails and a stunning meal I managed to put any regrets about no longer being on the Dream Team to one side. It was probably a good idea that I did not stay at the hotel that night because with my new-found empathy with the staff, I would have had to sleep on the floor and I certainly couldn't have had a wash. It was probably time, I got to thinking, for me to find another New York job.

2

Making a Boo Boo

As a Park Ranger in Central Park

*Y*ou know that game show on television called *Family Fortunes* which is based on survey results? It's the one featuring questions that start with the phrase, 'We asked one hundred people . . .' I am not a gambling woman but if they were asking the survey group the question, 'What's the most common event in Central Park?' I would put money on the prediction that the vast majority would say, 'A mugging.' The standard British view of New York is simple: it's a big place with tall buildings and a large park where people go to have their credit cards redistributed. Our commonly held belief is that Central Park is more like an urban war zone than a recreational space and that only crazy people wearing full body armour venture inside its gates. Central Park, as far as most British people are concerned, is just a crime scene waiting to happen. Consequently, if you asked the same one hundred people if they would like to work there, at least ninety-nine would say, 'No chance.' Call me crazy but *I* said, 'No problem,' because I felt like trying a New York job which involved relatively fresh air. Also I knew I only had $4 and a used one-day Travelcard in my purse.

The thing is, those ninety-nine British people and I were completely misinformed about Central Park because it is visited by sixteen million people every year and almost all of them leave with their wallets and health intact. The park is a vital cultural and recreational centre for New Yorkers and visitors, and plays a huge ecological role in allowing nature to prosper in the middle of this enormous city. It also, quite literally, helps New York breathe because the concentration of trees and plants in the park absorbs carbon dioxide and other nasty pollutants in the smelly Manhattan air, and release nice, sweet oxygen back into the atmosphere. We Brits should feel embarrassed that we ever doubted the place. It's important not to get completely carried away because there is crime in the park but not excessively more than you would encounter in the rest of New York City, and as in any major city, neighbourhood residents and visitors have to exercise a little bit of common sense to avoid personal danger. Basic Central Park Common Sense Rule One: walking in the park alone at night away from the street and path lights is NOT A GOOD IDEA. I think if you follow Rule One you should be fine.

Another fact which many British, and come to mention it American, people have got wrong about Central Park concerns its history. I always imagined that as the early settlers spread out north on Manhattan, they had the vision to mark off a stretch of land which would remain untouched for their and future generations' recreational pleasure, and that virgin land has become the impressive slice of green stuff in the heart of New York that present-day settlers know and love. Wrong. Every single inch of Central Park is completely man-made and was constructed between 1857 and 1873 on a site which was originally an unpleasant expanse of pig farms, swamps and granite quarries. Even more incredible is that despite being a symbol of all things

American, the park actually owes a great deal to Britain. Calvert Vaux, one of the two designers, was English and the other designer, Frederick Olmsted, although American, was heavily influenced by an English park in his plans. However, it was not Hyde Park or Richmond Park which gave Olmsted the inspiration to create a green paradise in the middle of New York. He took as his model the People's Park in Birkenhead. And why not? So there is a corner of this foreign land which shall be for ever Scouse. It makes you feel proud.

I reported for duty on a bitter but bright February Monday morning to the Central Park Rangers HQ building at the North Meadows Security Center way up where 97th Street crossed the park. New York was shining in the intense winter sunlight and the park gleamed white with the snow left from a heavy fall a few days before. The thermometer was reading just over freezing but with the strong winds blasting across the open green spaces, the old chill factor made me feel as if I was taking a stroll across an Antarctic ice floe. Once again in my life I bowed in supplication at the altar of Damart, the patron saint of thermals, and prepared myself to suffer along with the prover-bial brass monkeys. On the positive side, I did appreciate the relative stillness and quiet now that I was completely sur-rounded by greenery rather than concretery. I had been in New York for several days now and already my brain was completely accustomed to the never-ending roar of traffic. It was only in the park with the trees around me muffling the urban sounds that I realised how loud that motorised cacoph-ony was. This being America where the fact is king, I had access to precisely the statistics I needed at that moment. I had in my bag a handy press release from the Central Park Conservancy Office which told me that there were 26,000 trees in the park doing the muffling and that the car noises were being replaced by the rather more pleasing calls of up to 275 species of birds which had been spotted within its boundaries. It felt so rural I could even try to kid myself that the plaintive wail of a distant police siren was actually the cry of a weird North American owl in some kind of pain.

The man who was going to show me the ropes of being a Central Park Ranger was no less than the senior Ranger himself. Shawn Spencer was a thin-faced guy in his mid-thirties proudly wearing a deeply unfashionable moustache and the green uniform and beige hat of his profession. It was the hat that immediately attracted my attention because I realised I had seen it before in a piece of American culture which had always been an important reference for me, namely *Yogi Bear*. The wide and flat-brimmed hat with a slightly pointed top trimmed with cord was exactly what the Jellystone Ranger wore. I knew then that I wanted to be a Park Ranger so that I could live out a childish fantasy. Who knows? Maybe Yogi and Boo Boo were hiding out there somewhere amongst those 26,000 trees. I decided not to let Ranger Spencer in on my personal excitement about his headgear and that turned out to be a very good idea. Shawn D. Spencer was a nice man but it was quickly apparent that he was not gifted in the humour, wit, eloquence or fun departments. This was a serious man who believed his job was important enough to merit a strange new form of the English language to describe it. Put it this way, he was the kind of person who called a spade an individual soil-breaking and dispersal device. Talking to him was like participating in a management training seminar, only without the laughs, but I needed to find out something about him if we were going to be spending a lot of time together. Shawn was almost a local boy made good because he originally hailed from

Syracuse in upstate New York. He had spent eighteen years working in recreational management in Virginia but had come back to his home State four years ago to take on the challenge of Central Park. He enjoyed his job here but admitted that he could not help hankering after the real Great Outdoors and described his future life plan with his own brand of lyricism: 'I want ten to fifteen thousand acres of land for proper multi-use management, allowing me the chance to do forest wildlife co-ordination, and offering opportunities for client recreation which can be both passive and active.' Wordsworth could hardly have put it more beautifully. For the moment Shawn was one of a small group of Rangers who looked after the welfare of the humans and animals in Central Park, along with the help of the Park Law Enforcement Officers who were a bit tougher than the Rangers, and the NYPD who had a precinct in the park and were the toughest public servants of them all. The Ranger job involved dealing with the public, acting as a wildlife educator, guarding and protecting the extraordinary numbers of birds and animals that lived there, and wearing that fabulous hat. I had no hesitation in signing on immediately. How many times would I get the chance to be in a real-life Hanna-Barbera cartoon?

Shawn showed me where the locker rooms were and gave me my uniform, including the hat, and a training tracksuit. I was so excited by my outfit I could almost ignore the state of the loos at the Park Rangers' HQ. The sign outside asked staff to take care of the restrooms. Unfortunately nobody had taken the slightest bit of care and the place was in a terrible state. Some angry Ranger seemed to have taken a swing at the wall with a size twelve boot leaving a massive crater and in the cubicle I chose there had been some appalling happening which had not been cleaned up. It occurred to me that it was not a good omen for the management of the park if the Rangers accepted this level of squalor at their own base. Shawn looked very clean and tidy though, and I could find no fault with his personal hygiene scenario as we walked over to the training area which was in a softball pitch in the north of the park. We chatted about the demands of the job and he warned me with relish that there was a forty-five-page book of rules and regulations concerning the park which would soon become my bible. I would be able to consult it to know instantly what to do if I caught members of the public having barbecues, swimming in a non-designated swimming area, eating the plants, behaving lewdly, attacking the trees, or committing any number of other exotic offences against nature. As we strolled towards the training area Shawn did set my mind at rest by confirming that the crime rate was nowhere near the horror stories I had heard back home, which made me feel a lot better. To really motivate me Shawn related some of the more interesting statistics at his fingertips about the people who visited the park. Apparently, 57.7 per cent of parkgoers visited in order to relax, and for just over twenty-five per cent of them their favourite activity in the park was people-watching. I didn't have the will to ask him what the other 42.3 per cent of visitors came to do.

Training to be a Park Ranger turned out to be a very exciting process indeed. I was part of a group of very young and very fit-looking recruits gathered on the softball pitch who seemed eager to learn and Shawn expertly taught us a variety of techniques we would need out on our park patrols. He started with the Heimlich manoeuvre which is the accepted way of helping someone who is choking. Americans seemed to be almost unnaturally obsessed with choking because every restaurant I had been to had a big sign explaining the technique to

Stopping the New York traffic with just the sheer force of my personality.
And a whistle.

Audrey Barratt, the lady who knew all about Michael Jackson's bed.

The view from the 32nd floor can be stunning, if you're awake.

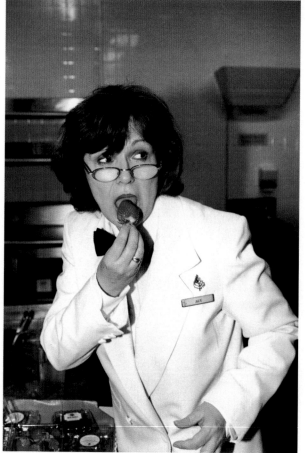

To me it was room service quality control. To Felix it was punishable by death.

Shawn Spencer getting news of a squirrel situation up in the North West sector.

Ranger Sal had quite an effect on me.

Shawn teaches me advanced Park Visitor interactive techniques.

Ranger Boo Boo.

*Ice Rescue was like
'Baywatch' but with
warm jackets.*

*Sandy Levine, boss of the
'most important Deli in
the world'.*

Oscar Lippi, the rudest waiter in America.

Jack Sirota, thirty-seven years and still going strong.

Margaret, proving that serving with dignity pays.

Susan, the Carnegie lady who knew what I was full of.

Working with Woody Allen at the Carnegie Deli.

'This is Julie Walters with Joyce Bellfield-Allen, for News Channel Four, looking the wrong way.'

Gloria Kline, always on the story.

Mike Hegadus sending condolences for the sad loss of Tape Three.

customers. Apparently if you are unlucky enough to find yourself choking you should remember to give the internationally accepted signal for the problem which is putting your two hands together and clutching your throat. I would imagine it would not be difficult to improvise that action even if you had clean forgotten it. We got to practise our new skills and my partner for the exercise was a handsome, muscular guy called Sal whom I got to hug round his flat-tummied middle and squeeze hard. It was good for me, I have to say. Then Sal, or Sally as I liked to call him, had to try the technique on me and as his powerful hands rattled my ribcage the chewing gum I had been chomping ferociously flew out of my mouth so fast it nearly lost someone an eye.

Shawn then taught us how to use the baton, which the Americans always pronounced with the stress on the second syllable making it sound like a kind of French bread. It was a shiny black rounded stick about three feet long with a stubby upright handle, and I learned how to threaten and scare potential assailants by swinging it menacingly. 'Get back!' I roared at Sal. 'I have a large loaf in my hands and I'm not afraid to use it!' He surrendered like a little puppy.

Shawn then took us all up to the Lasker Open Air Swimming Pool which, not surprisingly in the current weather conditions, was being used as an ice rink. We were to be taught the skills needed for ice rescue work and from what I had seen of the park, those were crucial skills to have up our thermal sleeves. There was ice everywhere. It was now around lunchtime and the earlier sun had disappeared leaving a kind of flat grey light which made the pool look like an Alpine ski resort before a snowstorm. I noticed that there was a strange flag flying above the pool building which resembled a green version of Canada's maple leaf symbol. Shawn, happy to be the fount of all knowledge, explained that it was actually a London plane leaf on the flag and it is the symbol of Central Park because it is by far the most common tree there.

Ice rescue turned out to have similar principles to water rescue, but was just a little harder, in every sense of the word. The basic idea was to throw a lifebelt to the victim marooned on the ice. Fortunately I had Shawn on hand to give me some expert advice about judging the target. 'Just picture their head and try to hit it,' was the pearl of Ranger wisdom he dispensed. I managed to chuck the ring close enough on my second throw for the poor, freezing recruit lying on the ice to get his mittens on it, then have the privilege of being dragged nose first across the ice by Shawn and me. This was a democratic lesson so I was the next victim. It was the perfect opportunity to do some Method acting preparation for the part of Jayne Torville's left skate in *The Torville and Dean Story*. Shawn also wanted us to learn the most elaborate kind of ice rescue involving a human chain of rescuers inching their way out to a stranded victim, then pulling him back slowly across the ice. He painstakingly set the test up, found a crazy volunteer to lie out in the middle, put me at the front of the human chain and set the rescue in motion. The problem was that the system didn't work very well. Every time I got out to the victim I grabbed hold of him passionately and then waited to be dragged back by the chain behind me. Unfortunately every time they tried, someone in the chain lost contact with the person in front, the chain broke, and I and my new-found friend were left to freeze on the ice. It was only on the tenth try that we got back to the side and I must admit I was quite glad. I had lost the feeling down one side of my body and my lips had gone a rather lovely shade of blue. Shawn was a perfectionist and if it took several recruits contracting frostbite to complete an exercise, then that was how it had to be. Apparently, being a Park Ranger was going to be no picnic, if you'll pardon the expression.

I was now ready to graduate as a fully fledged Park Ranger. I should point out that other Rangers train for rather longer than just one day but as a British television-type person I was being given special treatment and so I reported with a group of other undergraduates to the sheep meadow at the southern end of the park for the ceremony. The sheep which used to call the meadow home are long gone since their sheepfold was turned into the glitzy Tavern on the Green Restaurant. That's progress, unless you happen to be a sheep. I had to line up in full uniform, complete with hat, alongside fourteen fellow Rangers and Park Law Enforcement Officers so that we could give our pledge of allegiance and be presented with our badges by the Park Commissioner. All of my new colleagues were young and idealistic and I could detect a real sense of righteousness about them. These were people who were doing something practical about ecology and conservation in the Nineties and they felt pretty good about it. Behind us the New York cityscape crowded in on the park with the large red neon sign at the top of the Essex House Hotel burning bright against the colourless winter sky. A presidential-style podium had been set up for the Commissioner and we stood to attention as we waited for him to arrive. It felt as if it was getting colder by the minute and there was still no sign of the top man at least half an hour later. By this time the feeling I had lost at the ice rink, then successfully regained after applying hot fruit tea, I promptly lost again.

A flurry of activity up on the perimeter road set our minds at rest as Commissioner Henry J. Stern and an army of young men in suits descended on the meadow. Stern was a respected political figure and had already served time as the Commissioner from the late Eighties through to 1991 when Mayor Dinkins took office and promptly disposed of him. Now that Dinkins was gone and Mayor Giuliani was in power, Stern had been brought back and he looked as if he was enjoying the experience. Stern, an amiable-looking man in his fifties, had taken the liberty of putting on a jacket over his business suit to keep him warm during this time away from his large desk. Unfortunately the official-issue New York Marathon suede jacket was several inches too short to cover his suit jacket and his dignified demeanour was somewhat dented by the fashion result. His team of assistants all survived without coats or jackets despite the intense cold but there was a lot of frantic movement and swinging of clipboards amongst them which looked as if it had more to do with heat-generating than political action. I noticed that there were also black-jacketed security men with him who hung around menacingly, in case, I suppose, a terrorist sheep unhappy about the loss of their meadow attempted an attack on the Commissioner. The security men were not actually security men, I discovered later. Their jackets were emblazoned with the words 'Integrity Officer' which meant they would be helpless in the face of a terrorist attack but great at protecting anyone who was having their character flaws pointed out.

As a matter of fact, one of the recruits had told me that Stern was generally a good boss to work for although he did have the unusual habit of giving each of his staff what was known as a park name. It all started from the need to find distinctive names to use in radio communication but it had turned into an elaborate park ritual. Commissioner Stern had chosen the name Star-Quest for himself because Stern was the German word for star and he liked to ask lots of questions. So Star-Quest. I asked one of the men in suits, a rather plump, surly type, what his park name was and he told me, 'Marmot.' When I asked him why, he said, 'Because they are rather plump, surly animals.' I see.

The ceremony could begin. I attempted to unfreeze my lips from their fixed icy grimace so that I could make the Park Ranger pledge. Say what you like about Americans, they certainly know how to do good pledges. I was, after all, qualifying as a park-keeper but the pledge sounded as if I was being appointed as nothing less than an ecological superhero. 'I give my pledge as an American,' I mumbled that bit and crossed my fingers so it didn't count, 'to save and faithfully defend from waste the natural resources of my country. The air, soil, and minerals, the forests, water, and wildlife.' The words were so inspiring that all I could think of was that bit in the first *Superman* movie when the Man of Steel was asked what he was fighting for and replied, 'Truth, Justice, and the American Way.' Like Superman I felt that I had left my meek, mild-mannered other identity behind to transform myself into a Guardian of the American People. I had cast aside my ordinary clothes and donned the uniform and hat of a Green Warrior. Is it a bird? Is it a plane? No, it's SuperParkie!

Commissioner Stern then gave an inspiring speech peppered with British references in tribute to the new graduate with the red nose and blue cheeks standing shivering in the middle of the line. Central Park was, apparently, 'the Windsor Castle of New York's Emerald Empire'. I hoped that didn't mean there was going to be a terrible fire here which the New York taxpayers would have to foot the bill for. The Commissioner spoke with passion, and with tongue firmly in cheek, about the important duties we were about to undertake as newly qualified Park Rangers, like apprehending people who let their dogs run wild or kids who painted graffiti in playgrounds. He reminded us that we were not just enforcers but educators too, and it was our mission to teach New Yorkers about the herons, swans, geese, squrls and tufted tit-mice which inhabit the park. I was a bit concerned to hear about the new species discovered in Central Park until I realised the squrls were actually those cute little rodents with furry tails which we prefer to call squirrels. The speech ended with a tribute to the force I was joining. 'While New York City Police Officers are New York's Finest, and New York City Firefighters are New York's Bravest, our Rangers are New York's Greenest. You should be very proud.' If I had not been so cold that every one of my bodily fluids had frozen, I would have wept at that moment. Commissioner Stern then passed down the line to pin on badges of office and congratulate his new Rangers. He generously praised me for my training efforts and proved that I had truly been accepted as a Ranger by asking me what park name I wanted to assume. I had been thinking about this a lot and had made my choice after much consideration. 'Boo Boo,' I said confidently. All those memories of Yogi in Jellystone had confirmed for me what a great character Yogi's small sidekick was and I wanted to take his name by way of homage. The Commissioner didn't seem to share my love of cartoons because he had a bit of trouble catching my drift. He thought I was saying, 'Bluebird', then 'Blue Bill' before he realised exactly what it was I was suggesting as my name. His brow furrowed and he leaned forward to whisper to me, 'But Boo Boo means Mistake.' 'Oh yes,' I responded. He quickly passed on down the line after that and eventually the ceremony drew to an end. The Commissioner and his suits headed back to their cars and the new graduates dispersed to their new duties. It was now official. Boo Boo was in business.

It seemed to me that I had been trained up to be not so much a Park Ranger, more a lean, green, fighting machine so I was looking for real action as I began my first day on patrol alongside Shawn Spencer. Shawn did his best to dissuade me from any thoughts of excitement with his usual measured, some may have called it pedantic, approach to his job. He told me that he had made two arrests in the four years he had been working at Central Park. The first incident started out as a simple problem with a dog running free in the park, in the words of Shawn, 'A simple dog off the leash situation,' which deteriorated quickly to create a face-off with 'an irate dog walker'. The whole scenario spiralled out of control as Miss Irate Dog Walker decided in no uncertain terms that she failed to agree with Shawn's book of rules and explained that fact to him in a physical rather than verbal fashion. Rules then began to be shattered at an alarming rate and the perpetrator was eventually charged with Resisting Arrest, Assaulting an Officer, Disorderly Conduct, and not forgetting Allowing a Dog off the Leash. She would be lucky to escape the electric chair on that little lot. The incident had obviously left a deep scar on Shawn and he lapsed into an uneasy silence after he had finished the story. I didn't feel it would be right to ask him about the story of his other arrest so that had to remain a mystery to me. It could surely not be as dramatic as his first one. We walked in silence on the narrow tree-lined path round the Conservatory Pond at the east side of the park. The morning sun sparkled off the thin sheet of ice which covered the whole pond and I remembered from some long-ago reading that Holden Caulfield had visited this very spot in *Catcher in the Rye*. The park looked fantastic but in my new job as Ranger I found that I was now more interested in dealing with trouble than sightseeing. After an eternity of silent strolling I plucked up the courage to ask Shawn what might be the worst thing we could encounter on the day's patrol. He walked in silence for at least another thirty seconds before uttering the epic words, 'Good question . . .' and then said nothing more. I was beginning to get a feeling that being a Park Ranger and patrolling with Shawn Spencer would not require very much in the way of adrenalin.

Our patrol route took us towards the Bethesda Fountain which Shawn described as being the quiet area of the park. I wondered just how quiet a park could get. The fountain and terrace beyond it were meant to be the architectural jewels of the park but I have to admit they did not seem all that special to me. The location looked great though, dominated by the park lake and the skyscrapers on the west side of the park stretching above the trees. The spot looked vaguely familiar to me as many parts of New York do because I had seen them at some time or another featuring as locations for countless movies. In fact, the fountain area we were standing in had recently been the main location for the big abduction scene in *Ransom*, the Mel Gibson film which had just opened in London. The paths around us were now filling up with people and it was impressive just how intensively New Yorkers used their park. Everywhere I looked people were running, walking, cycling, skating, rollerblading, riding, and also strolling aimlessly which seemed to be a popular sport too. Shawn warned me that rollerbladers were often guilty of skating down the sweep of steps beside the fountain which made for 'a hazardous situation'. Not today though, because all the roller-bladers were behaving impeccably, unfortunately. I was hoping I could nick one of them for speeding but Shawn informed me that offence did not actually exist in his rule book. He did a quick bit of checking and discovered that I could arrest them for Reckless Skating or Being Drunk in Charge of Skates but I would have to catch them first and that could be a problem at the rate most of them were travelling. Shawn suggested the best thing to do was call the Ranger Rollerblade Unit if we encountered a law-breaking skater. That sounded quite exciting.

We had now reached the Mall which looked the most formal part of the park with its wide promenade flanked by tall elm trees. The place had a sort of Parisian feel to it and it was full of people sitting on long benches talking and smooching. I checked again and there was also no rule against that. One section of the Mall had become an unofficial rollerblade demonstration track and I marvelled at the skaters' skills as we patrolled beside it. Thirty bright orange cones had been set up in a line and skaters were taking turns to slalom their way down them. As this was New York, the correct approach to this difficult exercise was to do as many incredible tricks as possible but wear a facial expression which suggested you would have been more challenged opening an envelope. Talent only applied in this city if the attitude was right and some of the talent on show in the Mall was so impressive that even Shawn was moved to comment on it. They really were that good.

I was totally impressed until we walked a little bit further and I saw the Frisbee throwers in action. Now, I had always thought Frisbee was the thing people did when they had run out of conversation on the beach and it involved nothing more challenging than chucking a plastic dinner plate back and forth. Until I discovered the Central Park variety and my opinion was changed drastically. One couple in particular caught my eye. He was a short, very bald chap and his partner was a slightly plump girl in leggings and a tracksuit top. They might not have made the grade as cast members for *Baywatch* but what they were doing with their Frisbee was utterly stunning. The girl threw it with a peculiar twisting motion from behind her head which sent the Frisbee off at high speed towards her partner who caught it effortlessly on the tips of his fingers, then let it run across his shoulders, bounce up in the air, land on his stomach, run down his leg and then kicked it in the air with his foot. He caught it, whipped it back to her and then she began an even more impressive sequence of Frisbee juggling which involved her keeping the disc spinning off various parts of her body while expertly dodging people strolling down the Mall. I stared open-mouthed at this display of skill and athleticism but I noticed that all the New Yorkers around were keeping their eyelids completely unbatted. So they're good at Frisbee. So what?

Shawn had one more treat for me in such an action-packed day. He informed me he had to go off to the Park Ranger front line to do a class in wild flowers for kids, leaving me to do the final patrol on my own. The light disappears fast on a Manhattan winter's after-noon and before I knew it I was walking the Central Park paths in pitch darkness. All around me was the shimmering curtain of light of the city but the only brightness near me came fitfully from rather weak Victorian-style lamp-posts. I suppose, with the snow on the ground and the old-fashioned lights, I was walking across a Christmas card but the thought did not occur to me at that moment. I was petrified. The gentle beauty I had enjoyed just an hour or so before had turned into a sinister mass of twisted shapes and weird noises. Central Park can't be locked up at night because it is open at so many points and inevitably the place is inhabited during the dark hours by a strange collection of unfortunate people. I imagined that I saw every one of them lurking behind each tree and bush I passed on the way back to base. I got there in what was almost certainly some kind of record time and I have to report that I have never been so glad to see a filthy loo in all my life.

I didn't tell Shawn the next day that my final patrol had been a white-knuckle experience because I wanted him to believe that I was going to be a fearless Ranger, capable of handling any tree emergency or pigeon situation the Fates threw my way. He seemed to be in a more conversational mood so I thought I would try him on public lewdness which he had earlier hinted was a great area of concern. I wondered what the correct Ranger response was to the apprehension of members of the public in compromising situations. That is, finding people at it in the bushes. Shawn looked a little embarrassed as he took me through his rather headmasterly procedure of tactfully reminding the people that this was neither the time nor place for such activity, and requesting them to put their clothes back on and move to a more suitable location. I asked him if he actually tapped them on the shoulder to tell them all this but he said that he tended to turn his radio up a bit louder to announce his presence more subtly. Shawn could even make sex in the park seem boring and we continued our patrol in silence for a lengthy period after that.

We were walking alongside the perimeter road which took a six-mile loop round the park. It was open to traffic for a few hours every weekday to take the strain off New York's congested road system but it was open all of the time to non-motorised New Yorkers and there were processions of them travelling in every conceivable human-powered way. There was a sixty-kilometre road race going on that day so the road was filled with very thin and very unhappy-looking runners pounding the tarmac. I felt like arresting some of them for committing such an unfair assault on their own bodies but it's a free world and if they wanted to suffer it was entirely up to them. Suddenly, out of the corner of my eye there was a khaki flash and a speeding figure rocketed across our path. This brown bullet turned out to be Ranger Robert Vinci who was part of the famous Ranger Roller-blading Unit and looked like a cool dude with his beige uniform set off by futuristic black helmet, knee and elbow pads, and wraparound shades. He resembled James Caan in *Rollerball* and went some way to restore my faith in the street credibility of the Park Rangers. The Rollerblade Unit was set up after a girl was killed rollerblading in the park, in fact not far from where we were standing, and it had quickly become a vital part of the park safety team. I watched Ranger Vinci power off into the distance and day-dreamed about leaping on his back and demanding him to follow that reckless skater. I wonder where he stuck his flashing light when he was on a pursuit?

The patrol continued very much like the previous day until something incredible happened. We got involved in a genuine emergency. Shawn and I were down in the south-eastern section of the park when a breathless young girl ran towards us shouting something incoherently. She was trying to tell us about a man whom she'd seen lying unconscious out on the grass off the perimeter road. She said this man had his shirt half off and considering the temperature, that didn't sound good at all. I got so excited I could hardly think but Shawn barely reacted at all. He supposed we should get over there to check things out and started to amble in the right direction. I could not believe that he was taking it so casually because it sounded to me as if we were facing a real emergency and perhaps even a life or death situation. If a man was lying semi-naked in these temperatures he could surely die or he might be dead already. I felt a chill of panic spread through me as I pictured the terrible possibilities. Shawn's face registered no visible emotion but maybe he was panicking. Deep inside.

We picked up speed and were running as we reached the perimeter road. I felt a surge of fear as, sure enough, I could make out a man lying on the grass with part of his chest and arm exposed to the bitter cold. From a distance he looked completely still and I began to fear the worst. He might have had some terrible brain haemorrhage and collapsed in the park. As we got closer I noticed that he was wearing rollerblades and what looked like expensive sports clothes. Then I got the shock of my life as the corpse suddenly sat up abruptly and unleashed a stream of Manhattan invective at Shawn and me. I felt elated that he was alive but a bit taken aback that he was so angry with us considering we were here to help him. He was completely furious and cursed us and every other do-gooder who had enquired about his health for interfering with his right to privacy. He seemed ready to sue every person, including us, for causing him grief and was using words of one syllable to explain his feelings. When Shawn pointed out that someone had reported in good faith to us that he was in some kind of trouble, the man went purple with rage and I noticed that colour rather clashed with the blue of his shoulder which was still exposed to the bitter air. Despite the abuse Shawn was still incredibly unruffled by the whole affair and it struck me that his general lack of imagination probably insulated him from over-reacting to any incident. The consequences just did not occur to him. Meanwhile I was still lurching from the effects of seeing a corpse come to life, and the former dead body then threaten to sue me personally for millions of dollars.

When he had calmed down a bit he attempted to explain everything. It turned out that he had recently injured his shoulder skiing and his doctor had recommended the healing power of the sun so he had decided to do some sunbathing in Central

Park in February with the temperature around freezing point. Perfectly normal behaviour. He was surprised that people could think he was a 'kook or something' but he did admit that because he was growing a beard and looking a little unshaven it might just have been possible for someone to mistake him for a 'homeless' person. All this while he was still lounging nonchalantly on the grass. I was getting increasingly ready to put into practice the baton training I had been given a couple of days before, but Shawn diplomatically made our apologies and we left the man to resume his unusual medical treatment. I could not stop myself hoping he got a nasty dose of frostbite in that shoulder of his.

I finished my spell of duty as a Park Ranger on solo patrol round the park that afternoon and it appeared that I had definitely used up all my excitement quota in the Naked Shoulder incident. I might have had all that self-defence training but the most aggressive any member of the public got towards me was a raised eyebrow from a harassed dad when I failed to tell him which direction the zoo was. The most serious crime I saw being committed during the whole patrol was the wanton throwing of a Coke can onto the path, and I have to confess the culprit was actually me. I had been trying to throw it into a waste bin but I missed. Don't worry, I did pick it up and place it in the bin immediately so no real harm was done. I finished my patrol down at the Wollman Ice Rink in the south of Central Park where thousands of young New Yorkers speed round the huge outdoor rink listening to loud pop music and probably ignoring the stunning backdrop of familiar skyscrapers behind them because enjoying views is not cool. I loved the view, however, and staring at it hard i could make out the distinctive shape of the Four Seasons Hotel where I had been working such a short time before. It got me thinking that there had probably been much more excitement and nervous tension doing room service there than I had experienced in all my time patrolling Central Park. Still, I had got to meet Shawn Spencer and to wear the Yogi Bear hat so it had been worth becoming a Ranger. Until I had taken the job I had always believed that Parkies tended to be rather strange men who liked to hang around the swings a lot. I certainly remembered them being like that in Lightwoods Park, Smethwick. Now I knew Parkies could be a different breed of men and women with a noble desire to preserve their environment and probably the most boring job in New York. Personally, I felt a new challenge coming on.

3

If They Finish, We've Made a Mistake
The Carnegie Deli

*T*here is a very good reason for New York being able to claim the title of 'the City that Never Sleeps'. It is also 'the City that Always Feeds'. I have never been in any town where food is such a big deal and it is no surprise to learn that New York is, to use an American-style expression, the 'eatingest' place in the United States. In English that means the city where there are more places to eat per head of population than anywhere else. I was discovering that Americans do some strange things to our common language. If Manchester United were Manhattan United and as successful as they are back home, they would undoubtedly be described as the 'winningest' soccer team in the country. Anyway, it's hard to move for eating establishments in this city and they come in every shape and form you can possibly imagine. I thought it might be a good idea to try my hand at working in one of them because I considered that I was quite well qualified in this particular area of employment.

In my time I'm proud to say that I have, quite literally, served in the front line of the British catering industry. Years ago when I was a student I took a job as a waitress at the romantically named

United Cattle Products Restaurant in Birmingham. It was a Christmas job and it wasn't really a great deal of fun because the head waitress thought all students were layabouts and scroungers and she tried to make our lives a misery. I wonder whatever gave her that idea about students? There were a few bright moments during my time there and I do remember one special day when none other than the Welsh Lothario himself, Tom Jones, strode into the place in a tight-trousered way and asked to sample our fine cuisine. He must have been impressed by what we spread before him because he left a whole pound behind as a tip. What a life Tom must have had then. Monday it was probably coffee and donuts with Elvis at Graceland, Tuesday it was dinner with Debbie Reynolds at Caesar's Palace, Las Vegas, and Wednesday it was high tea at the United Cattle Products Restaurant in Birmingham. No doubt the days all blurred together in his mind and he could scarcely tell them apart. Or maybe not. There was one distinct difference between those glamorous venues and the UCP Restaurant. I'm sure that nowhere on the Caesar's Palace staff or in the King of Rock 'n' Roll's so-called Memphis Mafia was there an employee like Audrey who master-minded the restaurant menu. Years of experience had moulded her unique Midlands style of cuisine and her personal trademark, as I remember, was the permanent dewdrop hanging perilously from her nose. I'm sure that the dark and forbidding stew bubbling away on top of the stove sometimes got a soupçon of unexpected garnish which certainly gave a whole new meaning to the phrase 'Chef's Special'.

I decided that I wanted to experience a New York eating house which symbolised the city. Manhattan has some of the most stylish and expensive restaurants on earth but I believed that a more basic style of cuisine properly defined what the place was really about. To be specific, I was looking to find a restaurant where huge quantities of extremely fattening ethnic food were served at high speed by bad-tempered waiters. I think that kind of establishment would qualify as a candidate for the core of the Big Apple. Some of New York's restaurants are as famous for the behaviour of their staff as they are for the style of their nouvelle cuisine and I wanted to have a complete New York dining experience. I had been told about a place which allegedly had the waiter who had been voted the rudest in America so it sounded as if it could be what I was looking for. I found it at the corner of 7th and Madison Avenue and it was called the Carnegie Deli. This was not just any old eating house, because this was the restaurant which had been immortalised in Woody Allen's film *Broadway Danny Rose* and had been toasted by many experts as the quintessential New York deli. In other words, it served High Cholesterol with Attitude and it seemed to me that a spell working there would teach me a great deal about Jewish food and probably a lot more about New York people.

I had been issued the Carnegie uniform of black trousers, waistcoat, white shirt and black bow tie and was told to report to the deli at 7 a.m. sharp. New York was in the throes of the morning rush hours as I headed towards the Carnegie. The traffic on the streets was crawling along painfully bumper to bumper which meant there was actually more danger of accidents on the sidewalk where thousands of pedestrians power-walked at dangerously high speeds. I just hoped they were all fully insured. Everybody always seemed to be in some kind of a hurry in New York and it was hard to find a pedestrian who was not speeding. I'm sure that many people had a very good business reason for their aggressive haste and frantic behaviour but I personally put it down to the extra-ordinary coffee the Americans like to drink by the bucket-load. I'm not a coffee drinker myself but I had noticed that it acted like rocket fuel on anyone who started the day with a cup. Maybe if coffee was banned, New York would suddenly become a different place with relaxed people ambling down the sidewalks, stopping now and again to smell the roses, and with little knots of businessmen gathering to chat lazily about life at every street corner. Sadly, that was just a dream, so I had to battle my way through the flow of coffee-fuelled, grim-faced, dark-suited hordes charging along 7th Avenue to get to the Carnegie. The front of the deli looked pretty inauspicious and as I got to the door I noticed that another deli had set up just across the street. This competitor looked almost identical to the Carnegie except for a huge sign which aimed to lure people heading into their more famous rival. If imitation is the sincerest form of flattery then it looked to me as if the Carnegie was being lavished with the highest praise.

Inside, the Carnegie Deli had the frayed-at-the-edges look of a place which never stopped being busy. In fact, it was open for twenty-two hours a day and there was no such thing as a quiet time there. The deli was long and quite narrow and, I had to admit, fairly scruffy-looking. The décor was conventional New York deli dominated by wood-panelled walls made from the kind of wood which has never been near a tree, an open-plan ceiling with Richard Rogers-style exposed water tank and pipes, harsh overhead lighting, and a vague Fifties feel. There was not an inch of space wasted, either on the floor or on the walls. Cramped rows of tables stretched all the way back to the far end where there were a pair of battered metal swing doors into the kitchen. The walls were completely hidden by posters and literally hundreds of framed celebrity photographs. The photos were all of famous customers and the mix of previous diners looked quite bizarre. I did a quick sweep over the nearest walls and spotted

Colonel Oliver 'Fibber' North, George 'A Team' Peppard, Daryl 'Splash' Hannah, General 'Stormin' Norman' Schwarzkopf, Huey 'And the News' Lewis, James 'Sex Machine' Brown, Doctor 'What's your problem?' Ruth, Don 'Hairstyle' King, and Emma 'What's a nice English girl like me doing here?' Thompson. I could not imagine any link between that group of people other than the fact they had at some time been peckish and in the neighbourhood. I looked around the deli but I couldn't spot any celebrities having caffeine transfusions at that precise moment but it was quite early in the morning and I suppose there was still plenty of time for Emma Thompson and Don King to drop in and find themselves chomping sandwiches at a table together.

The Carnegie turned out to be bigger than I first thought because there was a doorway down on the righthand side which led to another wider room also packed with tables. Back near the entrance was a green-tiled area with a long food-serving counter decorated with hanging salamis and a big sign that advertised 'Cholesterol-Free French Fries'. I did find it hard to believe that in this temple to saturated fat anyone would really care about saving a little cholesterol, but it was a nice thought. When I had recovered from the concept of health-giving chips I couldn't help but notice that hanging next to the counter was the largest gherkin I had ever clapped eyes on. It was bright green, extremely fat, and a whopping three and a half feet long. Although it was a fake I amused myself by imagining the kind of Desperate Dan sandwich which could have been constructed out of a mega-gherkin like that. Then a waitress staggered past me holding up a plate which temporarily blocked the light and I realised that I was actually looking at such a creation. Loaded onto her dish was a tower of meat, pickles, and other nameless stuff which had obviously been put together using the Empire

State Building as a reference. I'm not saying it was tall but it was the first sandwich I had ever seen with snow on top.

As I looked around at the blur of frantic activity in the Carnegie and listened to the soundtrack of voices ordering foodstuffs I had never heard of, I suddenly felt incredibly nervous about working there. Waves of the kind of panic which always envelops me on first nights started to roll in. I was thinking seriously about rolling out the door when I was grabbed forcibly by a man in a white coat. This was Sandy Levine, the boss of the Carnegie. He was about fifty, tall and tanned with a shiny bald head framed by a band of white curls and he wore a white jacket uniform which signified that he was the top man in the deli. His face wore an amiable expression which he seemed to be trying hard to turn into a stern one and I had to admit that he looked the part as a deli owner. I was about to explain to him that maybe my working in his deli was not such a good idea when he began explaining the duties I would have to perform as a waitress. I think I managed to get out a strangled 'B – but' before he started his speech. Sandy Levine was a man for whom talking came easy and stopping came infrequently and this speech, delivered at high speed and high level, seemed unlikely to end before spring came along to melt the snow on top of the sandwich. Sandy would not consider the idea of my leaving before I started, mainly because he was talking so much that I never got the chance to tell him that I was having any doubts. He had the air of a man who had worked his way from the lowliest job at the Carnegie, probably the person who extracted the cholesterol from the french fries, all the way up to become the top banana or top pickle, whichever was most apt. As it turned out, he had only been doing the job for five years and got the post by marrying the owner's daughter. So much for my great powers of intuition.

Sandy decided that the most effective way of teaching me how to be a Carnegie waitress was to try a little roleplaying with him as an indecisive customer and me as a hopeless member of the waiting staff. I knew that I was not going to have to call on many of my acting skills to be perfect in that part. He began to machine-gun me with information about the Carnegie which according to his unbiased opinion was 'the most important deli in the world'. He told me that I must never forget at all times that the customer was always right which I freely translated as meaning that Sandy Levine was always right. He talked proudly about his finely honed system which kept the place open for business for all but two hours every day and warned me sternly that if I ever thought about not turning up for work one day I would be instantly dismissed. His general tone suggested that I should consider myself privileged to be working in such an establishment and that the honour of pulling on the uniform was almost reward enough. I begged to differ and asked him about rates of pay. Sandy gave a hollow laugh and told me I would certainly not be able to live on the money he was paying me for a basic nine-hour shift which included a one-hour break. What was this – 1897? Then Sandy explained that the real money in the job was to be made in the form of tips.

In America tipping in every branch of the service industries is a skill and the classic British attitude of 'keep the change' does not apply. Staff here have to rely almost completely on what a customer wants to give. A decent tip in a restaurant needs to be well above the 10 per cent we Limey skinflints might call acceptable and preferably should be up around 15 or even 20 per cent to get you out of the restaurant unscathed. It also wasn't unknown for Carnegie staff to get 30 or even 40 per cent tips. The equation was simple: I had to give the customers what they wanted in order to make them give me what I wanted. However, in a place like the Carnegie what customers were expecting was not necessarily a nice smile and prompt service because this was a deli which celebrated the fact that it had the waiter voted the rudest in the country on the payroll. I would have to serve the customers the Carnegie way and I was sure that it bore no relation to the way I used to dish out the lunchtime specials back at the UCP Restaurant. Sandy winced at my nervous and apologetic manner and instructed me to get myself an attitude if I wanted to have a future at the Carnegie. I looked him right in the eye and spoke slowly but with real menace. 'Worry not, Deli Man. J. W. is here to kick some Carnegie bottom. Now, let's get ready to rrrrumble!' Well, that's not quite true. What I said to him was, 'Sorry for being so apologetic.' Perhaps I had a bit to go in the attitude stakes. Sandy finished his beginner's guide to the Carnegie by defining the approach to customer satisfaction: 'If they finish, we've made a mistake.' This was an eating house where empty plates were seen as signs of failure because the portions were so enormous that it was expected no normal customer would ever get the chance to see if there was a pretty pattern on the plates. As a matter of fact, there wasn't, but there didn't need to be.

The Carnegie menu was a work of art. A work of abstract art, in my opinion, because I did not have the faintest idea what many of its entries meant. They appeared to be in a foreign language, mainly because they were in Yiddish. Words like lox, matzoh balls, borscht, knish and fresser stared up at me from the extensive menu and I realised that even if I was getting a 20 per cent tip I would have to split it with the full-time interpreter who would surely need to be beside me at all times. Bizarrely, the entire menu was also available in Japanese to satisfy the thousands of Japanese tourists who liked to visit the Carnegie. I wonder what attracted tour parties from the Land of the Rising Sun. I hadn't noticed any sushi on the menu so perhaps the world's most camera-obsessed nation just enjoyed being in a restaurant with wall-to-wall photographs. As I scanned the indecipherable menu it did occur to me that perhaps it would have been easier to work from the Japanese version than the so-called English one.

Putting my language difficulties to one side, Sandy thought it was time to test me out in the job so he presented me with the official Carnegie black order book and then acted the part of a customer while I played a nervous wreck. Sandy first asked (actually, demanded is probably a fairer description) for a Number Fourteen which was known as a Reuben and seemed to be a giant sandwich filled with an alarming number of varied animal by-products. Then he asked for a matzoh ball soup but changed his mind as he ordered it to illustrate the rule that every time an order was cancelled, the change in my book had to be authorised by a manager. He wanted an orange juice which was a command I felt that I could probably handle, then he scrubbed all his previous orders to demand a Woody Allen which was the pet name of the Broadway Danny Rose, the 'signature' sandwich of the Carnegie. It was a ridiculously tall multi-meat and pickle tribute to New York's best-known but very short director. Sandy wanted his Woody with some mustard on the side and also asked that I give it a 'shot', which was deli code for adding coleslaw to a sandwich. Mine was not to reason why so I painstakingly wrote all these instructions down in my black book and set off to the food counter where Walter the counterman and his merry band of counterpeople were poised to sort out the order for me. Remembering Sandy's insistence that I should become more New York in my style, just before I left his table I looked at him with narrowed eyes and spat out a tough Manhattan parting phrase, 'I'll just be two ticks . . .'

I quickly had to become acclimatised to life on the Planet Carnegie and the unusual customs practised there. These sandwiches I had been hearing about were snack food, but not as we know it, Jim. The Broadway Danny Rose was an extraordinary stack of wafer-thin layers of corned beef, pastrami, and processed turkey with sliced pickles between two tiny pieces of rye bread. It stood at least a foot high and held a staggering one and a half pounds of meat. The staff were told to hold these giant delicacies high above their heads as they carried them through the deli because customers liked to 'eat with their eyes' and would all be clamouring to order immediately they saw one. Have you ever suffered from the misery of visual indigestion? I hadn't until I worked at the Carnegie.

The language of the menu was proving tricky but I also had to face the challenge of coming to terms with the list of staff slang for key ingredients and orders. I had already discovered that 'a shot' meant coleslaw but there was a selection of other strange coinages. Pastrami was known as 'pistol', a 'combo' was any sandwich with Swiss cheese, rye toast was 'whisky down', regular coffee was 'regulation', and, most bizarrely of all, American cheese was known as 'Dutch'. I did ask why this code had evolved but nobody was very sure. It seemed to have a lot to do with the fact that all the waiters had to scream their orders simultaneously at the counter and items could be misheard. Pastrami could sound like salami, rye toast could sound like dry toast so I could follow that their code names would be useful, but I failed to grasp why renaming American cheese after another country made things easier for Carnegie staff. Anyway, I swotted hard on the Carnegie code book and soon felt completely at ease haranguing Walter and his team with phrases like 'Give me a pistol whisky down with a shot.' I just had to stop spoiling the effect by adding the words, '. . . if you're not too busy, I mean, I can wait if you like.'

When Woody Allen was filming at the Carnegie, no casting agency in the world could have provided him with as perfect-looking a team of waiters as was working in the deli alongside me that day. There were two women, Susan and Margaret, and it struck me that they both had a kind of quiet dignity in the way they held themselves. They were in control and efficient and obviously took no cheek from any of the customers or other staff. Susan was a tiny woman who had been working at the Carnegie for over eleven years and had the kind of face which spoke not so much volumes as the complete works of. She was in her fifties, maybe older, but had attempted to halt the ageing process by having some work done. Unfortunately, it looked as if the builders had left halfway through the job, and her face had the kind of terrible permanent grimace that only happens when they run out of skin. She might not have been a model for the art of cosmetic surgery but her eyes shone with intelligence and energy. She had very little advice for me except to keep sachets of sweetener in my pocket and to 'save steps' as much as I could during my shift, but there was a brief flash of her real experience when she told me I would only become a true waitress once I was made to cry by a customer.

Margaret was a much taller woman, also in her fifties, who had the concerned face of an infant school teacher and spoke with a soft, almost Southern accent. She had been serving in the Carnegie for over seven years and had little to say about how I should do the job although I could see that her gentle, almost maternal attitude to customers worked pretty well. There was also

69

a toughness about her and Susan which explained why they had survived in the Carnegie for the length of time they had. As I spoke to them I noticed that, despite the fact the Carnegie was predominantly a Jewish establishment, both women were wearing Jesus badges on their uniforms. I didn't ask why and left them to get on with their work as the deli began to fill up.

I did not have to ask which Carnegie waiter had been voted the rudest in America. I knew who it was the minute I saw a hunched figure shuffle between the tables muttering bitterly into his giant moustache. Oscar 'The Grouch' Lippi had a face which instantly reminded me of the innkeeper in Hammer Horror films. The one who tells the hero that nobody has gone near the castle for many years and then lapses into a strained silence as he polishes a tankard. Oscar had it all: the flat-top haircut, a huge bush of moustache which made it uncertain whether he had a mouth underneath, and one of those round rustic faces. All he needed was a pair of lederhosen and a cheap inn set in the background to really fit the part. However, in his real-life role Oscar Lippi was very happy being unhappy as a Carnegie waiter and took pride in his reputation for rudeness. As I had already discovered, America considered any '-est' an achievement and Oscar was delighted that his skills in bad manners had been celebrated. He certainly saved his rudeness for paying customers only because he was sweetness and light with me and seemed delighted to stop serving for a moment to talk about himself. He was of Scandinavian descent and had been born in Hoboken, New Jersey, in the same hospital as Frank Sinatra. There, it had to be said, the similarity ended. I noticed that Oscar's arms looked like the glossary to an atlas because he had lists of places that he had served in as a sailor running down from his elbows to his wrists, and I sensed the hunched way he held himself meant he had fought many battles during his life. Sure enough he reeled off a tale of personal medical misfortunes which involved heart attacks, liver disorders, cancer and a foot problem which made the miles of walking in his job a torture. Considering that one of the perks of the job was as much food as the staff could eat, Oscar was not the greatest advertisement for the health-giving qualities of the Carnegie fare. Unlike his colleagues Margaret and Susan, Oscar seemed to have been damaged in both body and spirit and had an air of sadness about him.

The other male waiter was a bear of a man called Jack Sirota with an extraordinary head of hair which looked as if it belonged to someone else. Usually in America hair that looked borrowed usually did belong to another person or animal and tended to be attached to the current wearer only by sticky tape, but in Jack's case the hair really was his own which made it all the weirder. He had been working at the deli for an astonishing thirty-seven years and was now sixty-four so he had spent most of his life on Planet Carnegie. Despite his length of service he had just one piece of advice to dispense to new waiters but it did make a lot of sense. 'Never,' he said meaningfully, 'serve prune juice to anyone eating here before the theatre.' Can't argue with that. Like Oscar it looked as if the years had not been kind to Jack and there was a defeated and unhealthy air about him as he lumbered ponderously from table to table. He did mention that he ate pastrami once a week for medical reasons, 'To keep the arteries open'. I think he was joking but I could not be absolutely sure.

Just to get things into perspective, the male waiters may not have been completely fulfilled in the job but they were very good at it and Jack Sirota was in the record books as the recipient of the largest tip in the history of the Carnegie, a whopping one hundred of those nice American dollars. Also the waiters had developed a computer-like calculating skill and Jack tried hard to teach me the simple way to work out the 8.5 per cent tax which had to be added to each bill. He proudly reeled off one of those equations which sounded considerably more complicated than the original calculation and I could only sit back and marvel at his instant accounting talents. What I liked best about the Carnegie was the sense of pride which I could feel amongst the staff. Americans have no hang-ups about doing serving jobs and it is in their nature to do any work to the maximum of their ability. I think that's admirable even if their primary skill is being rude to customers.

The time had come for me to do the job for real and I still felt more scared than was necessary. Maybe it was because I had a nagging feeling in my head that somewhere in a parallel universe there was a Julie Walters figure doing the very same thing. I remembered my times at the UCP Restaurant all those years ago in Birmingham and imagined how easily I could have ended up as a waitress if my life had taken just slightly different turns along the way. The daft thing was that most actresses tend to go from waiting tables to playing stages but here I was doing precisely the opposite. I had done the roleplay; now it was for real and so I headed off to face my public in my first performance as That Carnegie Waitress with the Funny Accent. I have to admit that I was not an overnight success and the critics were quick to point out that not only did I frequently bump into the furniture but I also did not appear to have much of a clue about the script. At least I knew that this was not going to be a long run. I had forgotten just how exhausting a job it was, being constantly on your feet and having to walk the same route back and forth from table to counter until it seemed as if I had done the Pennine Way but carrying a plate of soup. I also found the noise of the place quite intimidating, particularly at the counter area where everyone shouted their order to the counterpeople, most of whom seemed to be both South American and mute. There was a feeling of constant pressure on the waiting staff to keep the customers moving because if a table stayed longer than half an hour the original waiter had to share the tip on that table with another waiter, for some terribly unfair reason which I did not begin to understand.

I realised that I was now no longer an actor but a player in a true New York experience and I could feel my personality shift to handle it. Who can be polite when you have a deadline? It was hustle, baby, hustle and I had to shape up to survive. Unfortunately, I found it hard to demonstrate the right kind of sharply efficient attitude to my co-workers because of my utter incompetence. Even the simple things were hard for me so I quickly became the waitress who couldn't find any crockery when she needed it or didn't know whether to dress up for a matzoh ball or return it to the matzoh who'd lost it. At the same time I had to keep everything written down accurately in my little black book, do mental arithmetic for the first time in many years, deal with hungry members of the public, and cope with Sandy Levine watching my every move and passing comment. The concentration involved in keeping, if you'll pardon the expression, all those matzoh balls in the air was totally exhausting and very soon I had the energy and appearance of a wet dishrag. Still, there were only seven hours till home time.

The customers who visited the Carnegie were a fascinating bunch of people who neatly matched the style and ambience of the restaurant. They were business-like, predominantly Jewish, short of temper and time, and very long on opinion. It was inconceivable to them that a waitress at the Carnegie might not have personal knowledge of every item on the menu. Then I arrived. During the early part of the shift I got away with simple orders of items I understood like coffee and bagels but it was not long before the spectre of the Unknown Foodstuff arose to haunt me. Two well-dressed and highly respectable looking businessmen arrived and sat at one of my tables. I noticed immediately that they did not bother looking at the menu and that set alarm bells off in my head. They were probably regulars, knew it intimately, and would order something I had never heard of. They did. Scrambled matzoh bry and leo was the request and with nobody else around I had to shamefacedly ask the customers for a translation. The older of the two had taken a bit of a shine to me and so did not seem upset that he had drawn the waitress from hell. He told me that matzoh balls were large doughball-like creations which were served in soup or in various other concoctions like the one they had ordered. Leo was not grilled King of the Jungle but the acronym for lox, eggs and onion which was a popular Jewish delicacy. When I served the food the older man invited me to sit down and try some of the dishes with them as an educational experience. It was a tempting offer and because I was so exhausted I took a quick squint around to confirm that Sandy was nowhere to be seen and plonked myself down at their table. My new boyfriend told me that I should try the matzoh balls with apple sauce but just as I was tucking in there was a flash of white coats; suddenly Sandy was strolling past with a sneer on his lips. 'What is he,' he muttered as he reached me, 'a family member?' Then from behind me in the deli one of my new colleagues hissed, 'Don't sit with the customers,' and I realised that I was obviously committing a major crime in fraternising with the enemy. My boyfriend took exception to the treatment I was receiving and suggested that I should join the union as soon as possible to protect myself against the evil management. It seemed to me that I was in quite enough trouble already.

The stream of customers became a bit of a blur as I struggled to keep up with the demands of the job. I took a deep breath around lunchtime when I saw a couple of new customers at one of my tables, sporting the uniform of New York's Finest. They were identical in every detail down to their official-issue police moustaches and slightly shifty eyes. One wanted coffee and the other took tea which I presented to them with a flourish. The moment was ruined though when the entire cup of tea fell splashing over the black leather midriff of an angry New York cop. As my life flashed before my eyes, I rehearsed several options of my excuse before I realised that the cop had knocked the cup over himself. Being a New York policeman he had to pretend that the scalding hot tea had not hurt or affected him in the slightest but I noticed that his expression of casual indifference had become somewhat strained. I had another worry about dealing with my law enforcement customers. I had been brought up watching movies where the friendly precinct cop always dined for free in his neighbourhood restaurants and I didn't know if those Hollywood-style rules still applied in modern-day, real-life New York. There was nobody official around to ask so I did what I had always been brought up to do in a crisis. I asked a policeman. Both officers looked at me with casual indifference and told me that they certainly would pay but I could still not tell whether there was some kind of different message being relayed from behind those impassive eyes and moustaches. Money then certainly changed hands but I did notice Sandy chatting animatedly to both men as they left the restaurant. Maybe Hollywood still got it right sometimes.

My crash course in New York etiquette let me in for a real shock when a short, bearded, new customer said out of the blue,

'Cup of tea?' At least that's what I thought he was suggesting when he looked up at me, half smiling. I felt quite touched and almost took him up on the offer but quickly remembered my previous lecture about sampling wares with customers, and politely declined. My knight in shining armour listened to my sweet apology, laughed out loud, and spluttered, 'No, I meant *me*, not *you*, honey!' He then turned to his fellow diners and announced, 'She thinks I'm offering her a cup of tea!' I felt crushed and at the same time felt like crushing the customer's smug little face into the nearest matzoh ball. What was it Sandy Levine had said about the customer always being right? But only when the customer was not a low-life sleaze ball surely. I guessed that my reaction proved how well I was doing as a Carnegie undergraduate. Once he had stopped sniggering long enough to communicate normally with me, I discovered that he was a talk radio host on WABC from 4 to 8 p.m. every day. He seemed the right type for the job with his overweening confidence and non-stop patter. I made a mental note to avoid WABC at all costs. He insisted on giving me his card which revealed he was an iconoclast and raconteur but I thought that I should be the judge of that. As I continued talking to him one of the other waitresses walked past and whispered, 'You have other custo-mers,' with just a hint of venom. What a shame, I would have to cut short my chat with one of New York's great personalities and broadcasters.

Soon after he'd gone, still talking non-stop, I served a distinguished-looking white-haired businessman in his fifties. He turned out to be one of the top private investigators in New York. His name was Joe Mullen and he was private eye to the stars. He admitted to me that he had worked on cases involving Donald Trump, Johnny Carson and even Mike Tyson, but he would not confirm or deny involvement in New York's favourite relationship break-up story between Woody Allen and Mia Farrow. I was terribly impressed with his portfolio of cases. It was only after he had paid his bill and gone that it occurred to me it was not a very good trait in a private eye to tell a waitress in a deli exactly what cases he had been working on. Anyway, he should be enigmatic, have his collar pulled up high, and his hat pulled down low. He didn't even wear a hat.

The day was wearing on and I felt completely drained. The Carnegie was always busy but had its biggest rush from twelve to two and for those two hours I just did not stop. It was then that I met the worst-tempered old man it has ever been my misfortune to come across. His order was so complicated that I virtually had to guess what he wanted and when I delivered my version of his desires he was considerably less than impressed. He particularly did not enjoy having his cup of coffee served before the omelette which he apparently wanted as a main course. 'What omelette?' was all I could think to say at that moment, which did not seem to help matters very much.

Hour after hour I was having to serve these enormous meals with massively processed ingredients to people who wolfed them down with relish but I never felt in the slightest bit hungry. Like the sailor marooned on a raft it was water, water everywhere, but not a drop to drink. As one customer sarcastically put it when I expressed mild concern as he prepared to tuck into a sandwich the size of Wales, 'What do you know? British sandwiches are all teeny little things with grass in them.' He had a point but I decided that I would much rather nibble on a bit of lawn than half a cow when I was having a picnic. It seemed to me that the whole Carnegie attitude to food was rooted in the escape from poverty. People who have ever felt the pain of not having enough to eat tend to over-compensate when they find themselves amongst plenty and the Broadway Danny Rose was a powerful symbol of that acceptance of excess. I was not a big eater at the best of times but after a day living with the Carnegie menu, all I felt like consuming was a glass of water and a plain rice cake. They tasted better than anything Sandy Levine and his team could ever magic up behind those metal kitchen doors.

I finished my shift with a bundle of crumpled dollar bills in my apron and some faint and unconvincing Sandy Levine praise about showing some promise as a waitress. My accent had partly compensated for my incompetence but the Carnegie clientele had still been disappointed by my appearance on their favourite deli team. The truth was that I would never match the style of the regular waiters and waitresses there unless I spent the next thirty years or so living and working in New York. It would take that length of time to wipe away the last traces of politeness and humility in my character that would always mark me out as a loser in the New York service industry stakes. People are bred differently in Manhattan and I got another taste of the result just as I was taking my leave of the Carnegie. Susie the waitress came over to me to say goodbye and asked if I would ever come back to see them all in the future. Full of relief at leaving and knowing I would never have to work there again, I told her that I would love to come back to the Carnegie. It was the kind of ritual exchange people go through without really meaning any of it and in any other city we would have parted happily having completed the game. But this was New York and Susie had lived there all her life. She looked at me with that ravaged face of hers, smiled knowingly and said, 'You're full of shit.' Then she turned and walked away. The thing was, she was right.

4

In Sugarwalters, this is Julie Hill, for Channel Four News

NBC News Reporter

*S*o! I am on the way to being a Big Banana in the Big Apple, if you'll pardon the mixed fruit metaphor. A combination of the qualities which had made Britain Great had ensured that on the whole I had coped with the challenges presented by being a working alien in New York: grit, determination, pluck, endeavour, and a firm but probably misguided belief that the American Way which Superman believed in so much was completely inferior to my own West Midlands Way. As the old saying goes, 'When in Rome, do as the Smethwickians do. Behave exactly the same but speak in a louder voice.' It was that clever application of cross-cultural psychology which helped us British acquire an empire which eventually covered most of the pages of my old school atlas, and then lose it. The empire: not the atlas.

My next and final New York job was certain to be the toughest assignment of my Alien mission in the city. I was going to become a player in a cut-throat battle being waged every single day in New York with millions of dollars at stake for the victors. A battle which is being fought in the most public of arenas and which creates great heroes and villains overnight. A battle which is only part of a huge war which rages continuously between four giant armies for the hearts and minds of the people of America. Those armies are known as CBS, NBC, ABC and Fox, and they are the colossal networks which control the viewing habits of two hundred and fifty million Americans. I would have to go into this desperate battle protected only by lip gloss and hair spray, and armed only with a lap-top computer and a microphone. I was volunteering to work for television news in the most news-conscious, switched-on city in the world. A city where the News Ratings War is more closely fought than anywhere else in the world. And I was going in alone.

There may be no real blood spilt in the battle to be the number one television station in New York, but the campaign is fought with the smartest technology and the dirtiest tricks the media troops can lay their hands on. Television here is on a different scale from Britain and the numbers of channels and dollars associated with the medium have to be seen to be believed. British people tend to panic when they see the size of the American equivalent of *Radio Times* because it appears to be the thickness of a Jeffrey Archer novel (with better character-isation) but choosing a programme to watch is much easier than it looks. All the main American television networks seem to put exactly the same type of shows out at the same time so you only have to look at your watch to work out what to view. If it's 7 p.m. it's game show time, 7.30 p.m. is entertainment news time, 11.30 p.m. is the talk show slot, and so on. The concept of networks offering an alternative to each other would strike the executives here as plain crazy, so American couch potatoes have to accept variations on a theme throughout their television day or find their comfort in the bizarre world of Cable.

The network system is so fixed that it looks as if it was established by divine decree. Let the news be broadcast at 5, 6 and 11 p.m. and let it be presented by a middle-aged uncle figure alongside a good-looking young woman. And there were other fixed laws: it was compulsory to have a cheerful sports presenter with an eccentric haircut, a handsome weatherman with perfect hair, and an opinionated entertainment reporter with no hair at all. If a news show lacked any of these elements, it would surely fail. How could television executives imagine that their viewers were so shallow? Personally, as a sophisticated and discerning viewer I based my choice of news-provider on the quality of the signature tune. If I could hum it, that was the bulletin for me.

In amongst the identikit teeth and smiles of the standard cast on each American news programme there were actually some rounded, interesting people on show. They were the humble reporters who travelled the trouble spots of the world in their expensive designer wear, making sense of crazy situations in under two minutes and remembering to say their names at the end. No matter how superficial the packaging of the news shows, many of the reporters looked impressive to me and I looked forward to trying my hand at their craft. I know we were the ones who invented television news, but while we were still listening to dinner-jacketed announcers with a bag of plums in their mouths enunciating polite, uncritical stories about cabinet ministers, the Americans turned it into an art form. America created the image of the globe-trotting, do-gooding television reporter and the people who did the job were respected as important and valuable members of society with a powerful skill at their fingertips. Even in the cynical Nineties the profession is still held in relative esteem in America, especially compared to Britain where journalists have never been seen as particularly noble. Television news looked like the perfect all-American job for me. I didn't have the expensive dentistry work required to be an anchor person or the correct hair condition to talk about sports, the weather or entertainment, so it seemed that I was perfectly cut out to be a news reporter. I had even spent years practising the lingo, 'Julie Walters, News at Ten, in My Back Garden.'

Next thing I knew I was standing outside the Art Deco magnificence of the Rockefeller Center on 5th Avenue, home of NBC Television who were about to become my new employers. The Rockefeller complex of buildings is an impressive collection of Thirties architecture dominated by the huge GE Building where NBC are based. The sunken ice rink with the gold statue of Prometheus in front of the main entrance looked familiar, mainly because it regularly turns up in movies set in New York. I had read somewhere that the daily population of the Center was around 240,000 people. How very American to be able to tell most British people that your office is bigger than their city. I had been taken on by the news division of WNBC, which was the New York regional station for the NBC network and also happened to be the largest local station in the country. NBC was by far the most successful of the four national networks, and WNBC, usually called News Channel Four, was the market leader in the New York area.

My mouth was dry as I was swept by express elevator to the seventh-floor newsroom thinking what I might do to their precious ratings if I failed to do a good job. The newsroom area was being 'remodelled' so there was an unfinished and slightly chaotic air to the place as I arrived and it was also strangely quiet. I had imagined a place of feverish activity with men in eye-shades shouting, 'Hold the front page,' but what I got was a high-tech library with the gentle clicking of keyboards and the constant muffled ring of American phones. There were lots of televisions everywhere, perched on desks and grouped together in futuristic towers, but none of them had the sound turned up so it was very much like being in Dixons wearing earplugs. The newsroom was filled with people who all looked very purposeful in what they were doing and I noticed that none of them seemed to be smiling.

I had been assigned to work with a reporter called Mike Hegadus who was the feature man on the daily 5 p.m. bulletin. He did a sort of 'And finally . . .' slot called 'Neighbours' which was designed, he later told me, to 'capture the weirdness of New York, but with taste'. He turned out to be a rangy, slightly academic type who was distinctive for his very casual look in a newsroom packed with power-dressers. Mike proudly sported a cardy with a tartan scarf draped round his neck, an ensemble which looked more Nottingham Bowls Club than National Broadcasting Company. He was a veteran reporter with twenty-seven years of television experience under his tartan scarf and had been at WNBC in New York for just seven months. All of his previous working life he had been in Los Angeles so he was almost as much an alien in the city as I was. Mike was quick to admit that his type of gentle, human interest based reporting was very much under threat in modern news-rooms but he believed that he had survived this long because the audience response to his work was always so good. He told me that he was the last direct link to the community in a news operation which was becoming increasingly distanced from the people it was meant to represent. I liked him immediately because he seemed a decent man who actually cared about what he did and was certainly on no ego trip. Well, how could he be with a cardy like that?

Mike's righthand person was an extraordinary vision in bubble-gum pink called Gloria Kline. She was tall and had the constant broad smile and confident manner of someone happy in their work. The sign on her desk described her as 'Chief Investigator' and her job was to find and fix all Mike's stories for him. I noticed that she fussed around him like a worried mother. Gloria was certainly considerably older than him but it turned out she didn't consider herself a mother figure. When Mike was taking a call she whispered to me, 'If I was twenty years younger . . .' and her voice tailed off while she gave me a meaningful look. The cardy had obviously worked its magic. Gloria turned out to be a complete story in herself and I found myself practising my fledgling journalistic skills as we waited for the Morning News briefing to start. She might not have looked it but she was in her seventies and the very next day, 14th February 1997, was the fifty-third anniversary of her joining NBC. In an industry where programmes are described as long-running if they make it to a second series, Gloria was a piece of living broadcasting history.

What made Gloria Kline's long service even more remarkable was the fact she had sued NBC for sex discrimination back in 1972 along with another fifteen women employees. If the act of suing her bosses was not bad and disloyal enough, she and the women then went ahead and forced NBC to settle outside court for $2 million. The brave actions of those women helped cause a transformation at NBC and in the entire broadcasting industry. Until their success very few women managed to force their way beyond menial jobs in television but then the barriers began to lift and by the Nineties I could see for myself that the whole newsroom now was dominated by them. All these women owed much to Gloria and her sisters. Inevitably, NBC made the women who had rocked their male boat pay for their efforts and got rid of all of them. All of them except for one. Whatever tactics NBC employed they could never seem to shift Gloria. They even demoted her from her beloved Network News job to the backwater of Local News but unwittingly the move only succeeded in giving her a whole new career. When she arrived in Local News she was seconded to help a new consumer reporter called Betty Furness who had never done television and was deemed to be a no-hoper. Gloria then proceeded to teach Betty how to be a great television reporter and Betty taught Gloria everything about consumer affairs just as the subject became one of the most important on television. Together they became a formidable reporting team and Gloria truly had the last laugh on her employers. Twenty-five years after the lawsuit she is still a permanent fixture in the NBC newsroom and has recently been awarded an Emmy for her services to news coverage. I took to her immediately because she was intelligent, full of life, and really quite sweet! However, the news director who was brave enough to tell Gloria it was time to pick up her pension had not yet been born.

The story which Gloria and Mike wanted me to cover was apparently a feel-good piece about an apartment block in the Sugarhill area of Harlem where many of the residents were retired musicians and performers. The story had to be sold first to the news director of the morning meeting and Gloria took me to the windowless conference room where all the news stories of the day were decided. There were about twenty people sitting round a huge boardroom table but my eye was immediately drawn to the tall black woman sitting at the far side of the table. It was obvious she was the authority in the room and her quiet voice had the power to hush the general hubbub at will. Paula Walker had the look of a woman who did not suffer fools, or English actresses trying to be reporters, gladly. I sat quietly next to Gloria as the meeting flowed on with producers and reporters coming in to show their wares. Paula herself was in the middle of explaining the value of a local hospital story which sounded to me as if it could have slotted into any British regional news programme, when a tall, preppy-looking man burst into the room. He must have been very important or very stupid because he completely ignored the fact that Paula was talking and launched into a feverish speech. He was terribly agitated and all I could make out was that it was about someone called Miller and everything being ready to go. I waited with bated breath for Paula to shoot him out of the sky but she seemed happy to be so rudely interrupted and let him blurt it all out. One of the reporters sitting next to me whispered that all this fuss was about an 'up and coming mobster' who had been trailed by one of the WNBC newsmen and who had ended up threatening the reporter on tape. I noticed that the first question on all his colleagues' lips was not about the reporter's safety but whether these hot scoops happened while the camera was running. When they found out every gory detail was on videotape everyone breathed a sigh of relief, safe in the knowledge that one of their colleagues had done great work while incurring the wrath of the kind of man who could easily arrange for horses' heads to appear under the duvets of his choice. I filed a mental note about journalists and the milk of human kindness at that point. The preppy man was really animated by now and re-created the mobster's fury in full De Niro mode. 'You think you got trouble before. . . . Now, you really got trouble!' He paused for dramatic effect and looked straight at Paula Walker as he shouted the all-important punch line to the story, 'And we hear it and see it!' He stopped expectantly and she gave a tiny nod of her head. He turned and left the room beaming with pride.

The meeting quietened down after that but the excitement was not over. New York is a dramatic city and there were more stories pitched to Paula in the next hour or so which could have kept the scriptwriters of *NYPD Blue* busy for a month, particularly news of some shootings in the Bronx. But what I discovered at the news meeting was that there was one news story which the people of WNBC loved more than any other. It was the only story which could instantly guarantee higher ratings and was not about violence, crime, fame, scandal, war, politics, religion, or even the most holy of American concerns, sport. The ultimate broadcasting lethal weapon turned out to be The Weather and the people at WNBC had recent experience of its power. In the winter of '96 New York was hit by a huge blizzard and the city was completely paralysed. There was only one way for the frozen-in New Yorkers to keep in touch with life and it was television. More New Yorkers punched up WNBC News than any other channel while the snowstorms raged and the team had been basking in the glory of record-breaking viewing figures for a whole year. The downside of the success was that the executives had become addicted to the glory and even on mild nights senior newsroom staff would look up to the Manhattan skies and pray for an inch or two of the white stuff.

It so happened that I had arrived at WNBC on a freezing but cloudless February day with a sky which looked as likely to drop snow as I was to pick up a Broadway Danny Rose sandwich at the Carnegie. How did they put it so eloquently over here? It seemed to me that there were two chances of snow, slim and none. And slim just rode out of town. At least that was my expert opinion until a young guy with a checked shirt and a serious expression announced to the meeting that his computers were now forecasting a fall of at least two inches in the New York area around 7 a.m. the next morning. A real-life mobster performing on camera was good but real-life snow falling on the streets of New York was News Heaven. For an astonishing moment I thought that Paula was going to kiss the shy young man as he got up, unfolded his white wings, and left the room. Everybody started to talk at once and there was an air of genuine excitement through the team as they anticipated a day of bulletins which virtually wrote themselves and were avidly watched by millions. I could see reporters mentally checking their blizzard phrasebooks and polishing up expressions like 'The white stuff' and 'Snow go!' for regular use the next day. Today they would have to face the usual challenge of filling their shows with real news but tomorrow they would be able to sit back and let Mother Nature produce all their programmes.

Gloria pitched the Sugarhill story for me and Paula agreed to it with the slightly distracted air of someone who had her mind on higher things. She did, cumulo-nimbus clouds. I, on the other hand, had more earthly worries in the form of a commissioned news story for the 5 p.m. show, and no idea of what should be in the story nor at that precise moment any technical means of covering it. A camera seemed like a very good starting point so I was sent in the direction of a man called Tom Busby who allocated resources. Tom was a serious type hunched in front of a computer screen, who had the gift of being able to magic up a crew when a reporter whistled for one. He could promise me a one-person crew but only if I started saying prayers immediately.

I got ready to engage in some witty banter with Tom but with a gesture of his hand I was shown the way out and he began sorting out a genuine crisis.

I trudged back to my desk to prepare the story and as I walked past the rows of computers and monitors, all with a person attached, I felt the old opening night nerves begin to twang. On the outside I was playing the role of a WNBC newsperson, that is cool and relaxed unless talking about snow, but inside I was feeling increasingly nervous. It was the terrible inevitability of the clock which scared me most of all. Being a complete novice who knew nothing of the techniques involved in making a two-minute news report was scary enough, but the idea that I would have to do everything against the clock put me in the coldest of sweats. There seemed so much to do in such a short time. It was now mid-morning and I had to swot up the story, drive out to Harlem which would take an hour, record there for an hour and a half, drive back for an hour, and then edit it in time to go on the air at twenty to six. All I could think was that I would need at least a couple of weeks to achieve all that rather than the six and a bit hours I had. Everyone around me in the newsroom must have faced this torture every day of their lives and, as far as I could see, none of them were gibbering wrecks sobbing to themselves in the corner. I suppose that, as in every job, experience made the impossible seem easier. As probably the most inexperienced person in the whole of the Rockefeller Center, I, on the other hand, felt poisoned by adrenalin and had a strong desire to find a darkened room in which I could lie down for a long time.

Gloria helped me stay sane by completely ignoring my anxious babbling. All she worried about was getting the story ready and the questions prepared. I tried to read the thick bundles of cuttings she had presented to me to get some sense of what the story was about but all the information began to blur together in my over-loaded mind. I had always had a problem about reading quickly while taking in enough information, and that failing was coming back to haunt me. There seemed to be two stories, as far as I could see. One was the story of Sylvia Alston who had turned a rundown apartment block into an immaculately decorated palace that the locals could be proud of, and the other was about the amazingly talented show people, including Sammy Davis Junior's mum, who regularly turned up at the apartment. All I had to do was choose the best option, prepare the interviews, and get all my facts straight.

Gloria very practically suggested I call Sylvia but to my horror there was no answer from her number. I would have to call her from the truck on the way to the shoot so all I could do was hope very much she had not decided to go on any kind of day trip or things could get very embarrassing. I toyed with the keyboard of the computer as I put down some thoughts for the beginning and end of my piece, or top and tail as we reporters call it. Gloria had said something about Sylvia which stuck in my mind because it sounded poetic and I hoped I could fit it into the story. 'In Harlem the angels are on the outside of the buildings,' she said, referring to the carved pieces on many of the older houses there, 'but in this building the angel is on the inside.' Perfect. The one part of my script which I already knew off by heart was the tail because it followed a strictly defined pattern of words which I could not change even if I wanted to. 'In Sugarhill, this is Julie Walters, for News Channel Four.' I couldn't wait to say the line and I practised it over and over again in my head. 'In Sugarwalters, this is Julie Hill, for Channel Four News.' It would be all right on the night.

The sweet message eventually came through that a news truck

complete with cameraperson was on its way so I went down to
meet them at the West 50th Street entrance to the Rockefeller
Center. The sunshine of earlier had disappeared and the New
York sky was now dark and gloomy. It had started to rain heavily
and as I looked down the street I could see the bright red neon
sign for the famous Radio City Music Hall shining through the
greyness. I remembered that a few years ago I was asked to do a
reporting job for an *Open Space* programme back home but that
had only involved turning up and being handed a sheet of
questions. Now I was expected to fix a story, write a script,
organise a crew, direct the taping, edit the piece, and make sure
it got on air by half past five in the afternoon. It was now twenty
to ten and not only was there no sign of the camera truck but I
had not managed to speak to my main interviewee. This wasn't a
job, it was an elaborate form of torture, and I was ready to
submit. Mike Hegadus strolled out at that moment, totally relaxed
about the whole nightmare of uncertainty and time pressure
which made up a reporter's life. He had to face it every day but
the experience did not appear to have added many extra lines to
his smiling face. His face did visibly age a bit when he discovered
that I was ready to head off on my first story without an
assignment sheet. Mike politely suggested I might like to go
back to the newsroom and pick it up just in case. He said it was
an old reporter trick to know the address of where you were
headed. I saw his point.

The camera truck arrived twenty-five minutes late by which
time even Cool Hand Hegadus was beginning to fiddle with his
scarf. The truck looked the part though, like a large Ford Transit
with radar equipment on the roof and big News Channel Four
badges on the side. My nerves subsided a little when I met the
woman in charge of the vehicle because she was even more laid

back than Mike. Joyce Bellfield-Allen was an attractive black woman wearing a sleeveless jacket which looked like something straight out of the Vietnam War. I would have said she was in her thirties but she told me that she had been doing the job for twenty-five years so the strain didn't bother her either. She apologised for her lateness and assured me that I did not have to worry about anything to do with filming the story because that was her job. If it moved she would shoot it and make it look good. All I had to do was find the material for Joyce to point her camera at. We climbed into the van and my beating heart began to return to a more normal rhythm as we nosed out into the 50th Street traffic. It was ten-fifteen and twenty-five minutes later the paralysing effects of gridlock meant we had got precisely three hundred yards away from where we had started. I had lost the power of speech by this time so I had to listen mutely to Mike explaining how losing time changed a reporter's approach to the story. It would be up to me to lead the people I met to give me exactly what I wanted. He warned me that when you offered the chance to people to talk about their favourite subject, namely themselves, they did tend to wax lyrical. He told me that my mission would be to control them without seeming rude. It seemed to me that my mission was to prevent myself opening the door of the truck and hailing a cab to the airport.

Harlem is the most famous neighbourhood in New York and was named by the Dutch after one of their cities. The British in their time did try to call the district Lancaster but that name didn't stick, which was a relief for songwriters. 'There is a rose in Spanish Lancaster' just does not have the same ring, does it? Like Central Park the area has an international reputation for crime and violence which far exceeds the reality and as we drove north of Central Park into the heart of Harlem, the surroundings all looked fairly innocuous to me. The area did have problems but it was obviously benefiting from the rise in prosperity of the large numbers of middle-class African-Americans who lived there. We drove up Lenox Avenue to 125th Street where we passed the famous Apollo Theater, then headed further north on St Nicholas Avenue to the Sugarhill district. I managed to get my call through to Sylvia Alston on the mobile and she said she was expecting us any moment, thank goodness. I noticed there were some stunning buildings in the neighbourhood and as we pulled up at the location in West 150th Street I saw an incredible Gothic pile on the other side of the road which looked like something out of a fairy tale. It turned out to be the house built by Mr Bailey of Barnum and Bailey, and was a reminder of the time Harlem was the place where the rich South Manhattanites built their summer homes.

Apartment 62 was the address we were looking for and it was part of a squat five-floored block with a green awning at the front. Joyce picked up her gear from the back of the van while I smoothed out the creases in my suit and TV presenter hairdo which I had specially chosen for the day. I wanted to ask Mike if it was cool to be seen carrying bundles of notes but there was no time to question him because he was sweeping me into the building. Before I knew what was happening I was standing at the entrance to the apartment with Joyce behind me carrying a huge camera with a powerful light on her shoulder. 'Let's do it,' said Mike and I took a deep breath and launched myself into the apartment. 'Aren't you forgetting something?' Mike muttered in my ear just before I crossed the threshold and handed me one of those microphones with a little box which said 'News Channel Four' underneath the foam bit at the top. I laughed anxiously and prepared to enter the lion's den.

The apartment was long and narrow with a series of rooms off the corridor and a large sitting room at the far end. The whole place was filled with people and each room looked more elaborately decorated than the last. One room I passed, filled with African ornaments, had a huge ANC flag and pictures of Nelson Mandela while another was dominated by a huge old-fashioned radio which was pumping out jazz. I could hear different kinds of music coming from every room but the loudest sounds were coming from the sitting room where a crowd of people were obviously singing and dancing. I may have been gripped by fear but I could not help being influenced by the incredible atmosphere of the apartment. Everywhere I turned there were smiling people and I realised that I was seeing my story take shape before my eyes. All I needed now was to find the 'angel inside' and I would be in business.

Sylvia Alston turned out to be a slim, ageless black woman with fine features and a gentle voice. She had moved into this apartment six years before and had set about improving the place single-handed. She paid for wallpaper in the hallway out of her own pocket, then asked the other tenants to contribute anything they could to continue the work. The people in the block, who were mainly old people with very little money, gradually scraped together a fund which meant the whole place now looked immaculate. Sylvia had also spent time raiding junk shops to find objects to decorate her own apartment and had turned it into a palace brimming with interesting things. She was the living embodiment of the best kind of community pride and action and was a real example to everyone. As she told me her story I suddenly realised that Joyce was getting all of it on tape and this was being a reporter for real. Incredibly, I was actually enjoying the experience but just as I was relaxing for the first time in hours Mike Hegadus turned up at my shoulder to break the news that he had been paged and had to go back to the newsroom. He was having to leave me on my own to deliver this story and all he could do now was wish me luck. There was no time to sit down and weep so I had to keep working.

My next interviewee was Juliet McGinnis-Nelson who came from the landlords Friedman & Levine. The company had been the first ever black realty company and they were immensely proud of the work that Sylvia had done in the building. Joyce explained that Sylvia was not paid in any way by her company but they liked to encourage 'angels' like her to enhance their properties all over the area. 'In fact,' she said, 'they say the angels in Harlem are on the outside of the buildings, but in this one the angel is on the inside.' I couldn't believe what I was hearing. She had stolen my line. I felt furious until I realised that Gloria had probably heard it from Juliet in the first place and reported it to me so it was technically her line. Still, it would definitely be in my story and this was more than just a news story. This was a Good News story. The question was, would I manage to get the Good News on the air?

Sylvia took Joyce and me into the room where the music was playing and began to introduce the extraordinary cast of characters assembled there. The whole place was packed with people dressed to the nines, and every one of them was smiling broadly. It was as if I had suddenly walked into a giant surprise party being thrown in my honour. It was a pretty good place to have a party, as well. Harlem and music have always gone well together since the days of the famous Cotton Club and Savoy Ballroom, and this apartment seemed to be a meeting place for a large contingent of the people who had played a part in the long history of that tradition, though not, sadly, Sammy Davis Junior's mum as promised. She had not been able to make it along today but there was still a full house without her. Sitting at the piano was a tall distinguished man in his nineties called Morris Ellis who sang 'Ol' Man River' beautifully but very, very slowly. I was conscious as I watched him sing that I would have to cover the assembled crowd as quickly as possible or I would never have time to edit the story for transmission. There was just one problem. Every single person there had a story and a party piece and they all wanted to do them on television. But what stories. One man who looked resplendent in a yellow turban had been Ella Fitzgerald's singing partner in her earlier years and he sang a song to prove how good he was. A lady who must have been in at least her seventies insisted on doing some break dancing, and then there was a woman who sang 'On a Clear Day You Can See Forever' who went on to improvise brilliantly. She would have gone on Forever and Forever if I had not made a technical excuse and moved on.

Joyce pulled me to one side and said that she had been beeped by the newsroom to warn us that we should be on our way or we would miss the edit slot. I couldn't have agreed more so I marshalled every person in the apartment together and stood in front to do my final line. I was more used to the world of rehearsals and multi-takes but there was no chance in this job. I had one go and it had to be right. 'They say that Harlem isn't what it used to be, but I'm here to say that it is. In Sugarhill, this is Julie Walters for News Channel Four.' I could have wept with joy. Kate Adie, bloody watch it! I looked over to Joyce to get her approval but she had already disappeared. It was two-fifteen and the piece we now had in the can would be on the air in a little over three hours.

On the way out I remembered that we needed to get a shot of

the outside of the building so Joyce quickly grabbed a couple, then we began the journey south through the traffic-clogged streets back to the Rockefeller Center. The weather had improved a little but it still looked grey and unpleasant as we dashed down past Central Park. It was now two-thirty and we were due to be in the edit suite at three but there was no way we could make that slot unless we hitched a lift from the NBC Skycam helicopter. As Joyce weaved through the never-ceasing traffic I gripped hard onto the three tape boxes which contained the fruits of my labours and vowed never to criticise any television news reporter again as long as I lived. We got to the GE Building at three-twenty and Joyce dropped me off at the door. She was off to New Jersey on another job and I had to race to the newsroom to get to the edit suite. Mike Hegadus met me as I rushed in and he looked ominously serious. He told me that because I was twenty minutes' late someone else had taken the edit suite I had been booked into so I would not be able to begin preparing my piece for another hour. Another hour! He then told me in his laconic way 'to go cool my jets for a while'. My jets would not have cooled at that moment even if you had encased them in solid ice. It was now three-twenty-five and I had to turn the miles of tape I was clutching in my hands into a two-minute polished report ready for broadcast at five-forty. I sat down and stared out of the window clutching a foam cup of horrible American tea. How on earth could people do this job for a living? And more importantly, how could they drink this tea?

It was well after four when I finally got into the edit suite and I was by now well past the stage of caring. The editor was called J.C. and he was a pleasant young guy with a slight foreign accent and the air of a helpful librarian. I asked him if he liked a challenge and he shrugged good naturedly. He then asked me if I had my edit notes and when I said, 'Notes?' his face took on a more fixed expression. The edit suite looked enough like Mission Control, Houston to scare the life out of me and it was a relief when the calming image of Sylvia Alston appeared on several of the screens. J.C. and I watched her answer my halting questions and then began to pick out the bits which would fit into the final piece. I had a sort of idea of what I wanted the piece to look like and I began to feel confident that with the technical skill of J.C. to help me I would manage to achieve it. Then disaster struck. J.C. slotted Tape Three into the machine to find my spectacular name check tailpiece and seemed to have some trouble locating it. In fact, he had trouble locating anything because there appeared to be nothing on the tape. I'm no technical wizard but my expert opinion was that Tape Three was blank. As blackness flashed across the screens in the edit suite my whole life flashed in front of my eyes. I had got this far but I was going to fail dismally because of the most basic broadcasting mistake of them all, namely that I had reported the story but forgotten to press the record button on the camera. It was going to be hard to explain this away to Paula Walker.

J.C. checked the tape again and tried the other two tapes in case by some miracle the missing material had found its way onto them but it was no good. The stuff was missing and we were going to have to manage without it. I had rarely felt so despondent. Then the phone rang and J.C. listened for what seemed like ages to an animated message. There was good news and bad news. The good news was that Tape Three had been found, the bad news was that it was still in Joyce's camera which was now in New Jersey. Unless some miracle occurred to allow the tape to be fed down lines to us in the suite, I would have to kiss goodbye to my precious material. J.C. looked up at the clock which was now reading four-thirty-five and suggested that I should now begin to improvise if I wanted to get something on the air by five-forty. I tried to offer some ideas of bits we could cobble together to salvage the story. He dutifully pressed his console and stuck together some chunks of interview but I could sense he felt he was on a sinking ship with a captain who was not in control. At five to five I asked him how much we had assembled on tape so far and he clicked a few buttons. 'Four seconds,' he said quietly and I felt my head swim. Fifteen minutes later we now had a grand total of thirteen seconds on tape and I was preparing my NBC resignation speech. Then the phone rang and the suite became a blur of activity. The miracle had come to pass and they were sending Tape Three down the line to us. I watched in sheer delight as I saw my closing piece appear on the monitor in front of me. When the going gets tough, the novices get even more useless so I sat in complete silence as J.C. worked like a man possessed for the next fifteen minutes. Suddenly he was handing me a tape and shouting at me to get it to the studio. The next few moments were very like that scene in *Broadcast News* when the tape is rushed through the building to make transmission by the skin of its teeth. I hustled out of the suite, found a man with an outstretched arm and threw the tape at him. Then I leaned against the wall shaking with nerves. All I had to do now was watch the result.

Seconds later I was standing beside Gloria, Mike, and the imposing figure of Paula Walker in front of a bank of about twelve screens, one of which was playing the WNBC Five O'clock News. Bizarrely, I spotted that one of the other screens seemed to be showing a programme about the former Prime Minister Harold Wilson so it was Wilson and Walters sharing top billing as we both attempted to entertain the people of New York. I was so drained of emotion by the rigours of the day that I could hardly take in what I was watching. Before I knew it the smiling news show presenters were introducing my report and then for one minute twenty-eight seconds I was broadcasting to New York's largest news audience. It was all there: Sylvia, Juliet, the shot of the building, the turban, Morris and 'Ol' Man River', the senior citizen break dancing, and little old me saying, 'In Sugarhill, this is Julie Walters, for News Channel Four.' Then the faces of the smiling presenters were back on screen introducing the weatherman and I was broadcasting history. I looked up at the six-foot figure of Paula Walker and her face betrayed no emotion. She did not speak for a long time, then without a flicker of emotion on her face turned to me and said, 'Pretty good.' I did not know whether to laugh or cry but before I could choose she helped me select the right option: 'Don't hold the microphone so close to your mouth, you're not at a pop concert.' She paused, then fixed me with a steely glare. 'Yes, perfectly respectable,' she started to smile as she talked, 'but not good enough for New York.'

I left WNBC physically and emotionally spent after running on pure adrenalin since the crack of dawn. I realised that learning a job as intense and complex as this in the space of one day was almost impossible but I would have a considerably better idea of what to do if I ever tried it again in the future. I doubted very much if I ever would because I knew deep down I wasn't really cut out for this kind of work. It took a special type of person to face the rigours of hitting the air on time every day and the strain would probably be too much for me because we do have a history of heart trouble in our family. I had given WNBC my best shot but learning the job in one day was no way to make a Barbara Walters out of a Julie Walters. It felt like time to move on in my American voyage. As they say in the trade I had just failed the apprenticeship for, 'In New York, this is Julie Walters, for not very much longer.'

I slept badly that night, dreaming that I was trapped in an infernal edit suite with the hands of the clock above my head spinning faster and faster as a mad editor who looked like a cross between Shawn Spencer and Sandy Levine roared at me. I could hear the honeyed voices of the smiling presenters introducing my report which was still lying in bits on the floor and just as Paula Walker loomed above me I woke with a sudden start. It was all a terrible nightmare, thank goodness. The alarm clock by my bed was reading just after 7 a.m. and before I turned over to get back to sleep I remembered that seven was the zero hour for Winter Wonderland, according to the WNBC weatherman during the news meeting. I went to the window ready to enjoy the shining white beauty of an Alpine Manhattan but to my surprise the streets were black with traffic and the sky was dispensing dirty rain rather than fluffy snowflakes. I reached for the remote and clicked on the WNBC Morning News show which was filled with reporters standing beside free-flowing Expressways with embarrassed looks on their faces and very little to say. Even the smiling presenters' perfect lips were quivering as they introduced reporter after reporter with nothing to report. I may have experienced a nightmare but I got to wake up from mine.

PART TWO

Miami

5

You Are Now Entering a
Clothing Optional Area
With the Miami Police

he second phase of my crash course in the Real America started with a cab ride back through the mean streets of Manhattan out to JFK Airport. I felt sad to be leaving New York because the truth is that after a few days the city gets into your system and you become addicted. I felt like a New Yorker as the cab nosed its way through the motorised war zone they call rush hour. And I found myself referring to people as 'assholes'. Up until getting in the cab that word had never ever passed my lips. All right, that's a lie. Well, I might have said it once or twice, but always with very good reason and I always said sorry afterwards. Now I was being gratuitously offensive *and* not apologising. I was turning into Julie De Niro. 'You talkin' to me . . . ?'

The contrast between the journey from JFK into Manhattan and the trip out again could not have been more marked. The breathtaking drama of the first sight of the man-made mountain range of skyscrapers was replaced by the never-changing vista of boring Anytown suburbs, or at least as much of them as I could see beyond the crimson and rather hairy expanse of my cab driver's neck. Actually, after staring at his rear view for long enough I began to realise that his head was shaped quite like the Chrysler Building, but not as beautiful. We arrived at the airport just as the dazzling winter sun was going down in a blaze of smog-induced Technicolor splendour over Manhattan. I opened the cab door and felt the February chill catch me. It was just above freezing by then and as I paid the driver and headed into the terminal building I took my last fix of the sharp New York air which stung your face and burned your lungs. The intensity of my Manhattan adventure had left me feeling almost at peace and vaguely spiritual and I wanted to enjoy the final seconds of my time there. I looked back across the darkening spread of tarmac outside the terminal throbbing with cars and people and caught a glimpse of my cab driver sitting motionless in a line of traffic almost as if he had been frozen in time. He glanced up at that moment, saw me in the distance and lazily raised a leather-clad arm in farewell. It was a poetic moment and I searched for the right word to capture the instant. 'Asshole,' I whispered. Maybe it *was* time for me to get out of this city.

I did have a ticket to ride and my destination was the Sunshine State, Florida. It was not a place I knew a great deal about because I had only been there briefly once before, ten years ago. I had just done *Educating Rita* and Burt Reynolds, yes *the* Burt Reynolds, got terribly keen that I appear in a film of his called *Stick.* He insisted I fly down to Miami from New York, then flew me in his helicopter to his house where he attempted to convince me to be in his movie. Burt was extremely nice and very persuasive but I managed to resist his offer. I had just a couple of small reasons for saying no, namely it was a terrible part and an awful script, but that seemed enough for me at that stage in my career. So all I knew about Florida was that it was the

Making up the numbers at the Metro Dade Police School.

High-speed bird-racing action live from Miami.

The Beach Bill: with
Sergeant Tom
Buchanan and Officer
Kurt Brauty.

The Mayor of Haulover
Beach in his official
robes.

'Just how strong is that black tape?'

No Pesky Critter could rest easy. Todd Hardwick and assistant.

Face to face with the goat from hell.

'I've found the end!'

Carolyn Miller takes me on a journey through space at the Moss House.

Carlos Justo puts his arm round another unsuspecting victim.

The Shah of Iran's sister's house. '$7.9 million for this?'

An Alien phones home for the last time.

only State in the Union where Mickey Mouse and vicious drug barons feel equally at home. I'm not exactly sure but I don't think that's a positive quality about the place. As I flew the thousand miles south from New York, I was about to discover that Florida is a different State where everything is in a different state, if you catch my drift. It was February and New York was freezing with snow showers but in Miami the temperature was in the high seventies with bright sunshine; it was America but in Miami the predominant language was Spanish; and it was Monday but in Miami everyone was only interested in *mañana*. There was one aspect which was the same: a dollar was worth exactly the same in Miami as it was in New York. It was time for me to go to work to earn some.

I arrived in Miami late in the evening dressed, of course, for the Manhattan chill and as I waited for my luggage to lurch past me on the carousel I decided that I had made a good clothes choice. Miami International Airport was absolutely freezing. The baggage claim area felt like Platform four at Crewe Station on a frosty Tuesday in December. Thank goodness for my woollen overcoat with tasteful fur (false, if you please) collar, I thought to myself as I retrieved my case from the conveyor belt and set off to find a cab. The automatic doors hissed open and I stepped out of the airport and into the oven of a Miami night. Someone had set the place to Gas Mark 6; a little sprinkling of rosemary and I'd be perfect. I headed for the glorious chill of an air-conditioned cab where I could scrunch my coat up into a tiny carrier bag and pretend that I was perfectly prepared for South Florida. Welcome to Miami.

Greater Miami has a population of about two million people and the important thing I had to know about them was that half of that number thought I spoke with a funny accent and the other half thought I spoke with a funny accent and in a funny language. A million Miami residents think English is a foreign tongue despite calling America home and the city is filled with the sound of Spanish on the streets, on the radio and the television, everywhere. The United States has around a ten per cent Hispanic population but in Miami that figure is nearly fifty per cent. They call Miami the capital of Latin America and it is not difficult to see and hear why. There are immigrants here from every Central and South American country and from all over the Caribbean, and they have brought the tastes, colours, rhythms and style of their homelands to give the city a character unique in North America. I loved the intoxicating mix of influences but it could all have been so different for Florida because *we* used to own the place. Florida had the great good fortune to be a British colony from 1763 to 1783 when we decided to swap it with the Spanish for the Bahamas. I'm not sure why, because the government certainly did not have another Florida in their colonies collection. Anyway, the sad fact is that now our only official claim to the place is that Michael Caine has just opened a restaurant on South Beach.

The dominant immigrant influence in Miami is without doubt provided by the Cubans. There are around 600,000 of them in the area, all refugees from Fidel Castro's Caribbean communist experiment which has been going for nearly forty years. Hundreds of thousands of non-believers have escaped to Miami where many have become tremendously successful and contributed hugely to the growth of the city. Even newly arrived, I could sense the Cuban influence which filled the streets of Miami with Latin colour, sounds, and smells. This was an American city where people seemed more interested in news from Havana than from Washington and it was possible to walk down street after street of shops where they would only talk to you in Spanish. I was already an Alien in America but here I felt like an alien Alien. It was probably a good idea for me to brush up on my salsa skills.

I woke early my first morning in Miami and knew immediately that I had left New York far behind me. The sun was just rising but already the temperature was in the seventies and a gentle aromatic breeze was tugging at the curtains. I could hear traffic sounds but rather than the concentrated assault of the Manhattan Motor Symphony, I was conscious of just the low distant hum of contented commuters driving trouble-free through the sunshine. I looked out of the window and saw groves of cypress and jasmine trees, lush green lawns, and the morning sunshine dancing on an azure and white swimming pool. I picked up a glass of orange juice and blinked in surprise as the freshest citrus flavour I had ever experienced burst on my tongue. Someone on the radio was saying that it was definitely going to be a good day, probably getting to 78 degrees later, with a zero per cent chance of rain. For a very pleasurable moment I thought I might be in heaven, then I remembered something important. The police wanted to see me at 7 a.m. sharp.

Miami has always had a lot going for it, as I had witnessed that morning, but it also had problems. The British have for a long time been regular visitors to the city but in recent years many of them have felt the need to pack a bullet-proof vest along with the Union Jack shorts and knotted hankies after a spate of tourist robberies and murders. Miami actually had the dubious distinction back in 1981 of becoming the Murder Capital of the USA when 621 people died violently. Crime, sadly, is very much part of a Miami heritage stretching back to the 1930s when none other than Al Capone came down to Florida for a while to grab some rays and kill people. From his luxurious headquarters in the stylish Biltmore Hotel he behaved very much as he had done in Chicago and took over the running of all the illegal activities in the city. Sixty years later crime has moved into a scale which would have scared even Al Capone and all because of one particular illegal activity. Drugs. This scourge has affected Miami life for years, causing hundreds to be murdered, and generating unbelievable riches for the criminals. Someone told me that the drugs smuggling industry was now turning over something like $12 billion a year. Twelve billion? You could really put a man on the moon for that money rather than him just thinking he was on the moon. In the last few years there has been a backlash against this tidal wave of crime and the Miami and Dade County Police were playing a huge part in halting the terrible downward spiral of the area. It was a dirty job, but someone had to do it. Me.

I reported to the Dade Police School of Justice and Safety Administration just before seven o'clock to learn how to fight crime in Miami. The idea was that I would spend a few hours mastering the techniques, then be unleashed on the bad guys of South Florida. I was sure that they would be quaking in their designer boots at the prospect. The police school was out in the north suburbs of the city and looked like a British technical college but with a lot more uniforms around. I was given a white T-shirt with my surname and two zeros emblazoned on the front and back, a pair of black shorts, and told to get ready for a run. In a police car, I confidently supposed until I saw my thirty-five fellow recruits line up outside the front door. We were going to run using our legs and it wasn't even 7.30 a.m. Well, it hadn't taken me long as a police officer to find some criminal activity.

The recruits formed up into three columns and we were guided out by a short, extremely muscular guy with the loudest voice I had ever heard. Now, I'd seen all those American movies set in army training camps and enjoyed the way the soldiers always manage to sing those clever rap songs as they run along at full speed. I didn't ever imagine that I would end up myself in the middle of a column of finely trained personnel attempting to run and sing in tune and on the beat. But there I was puffing up a Miami dual carriageway trying to remember the words to a song which was being shouted at me by a mean-looking recruit. It went something like this: 'Woke up this morning with the rising sun . . .' which was an absolutely correct fact, 'Gonna run all day till the running's done . . .' which was a very frightening one. If we didn't stop soon then the only crime I would be experiencing would be against my lungs and knees and would possibly end up in an arrest. A cardiac one. Luckily, we turned at that point and ran back into the college before I embarrassed myself. My fellow recruits were a complete mix of sex, race and physical build but one shared aspect that I noticed as we went through a military-style falling out ceremony was that everyone was quite short. I always thought you had to be tall to be a cop but there was no heightism on show here.

The chief instructor was Officer Bill Dwyer, a heavy-set man in his late forties and a Vietnam veteran. He had the kind of close-cropped moustache that a huge number of American policemen like to sport and the taches all looked so similar that I wondered if they were standard issue. Bill ran with us but I was pleased to notice that for an instructor he seemed considerably more unfit than I was. He was sweating profusely and that was before we started running, and he had a tummy which had been conditioned by Budweiser. Panting, he threw me a navy blue tracksuit and told me to report to the gym which was a windowless hall on the first floor of the college and it reminded me of every school gym I had ever been in. The recruits lined up in navy blue ranks and prepared to be beaten into shape by a collection of noisy, red-shirted instructors. My fellow recruits were all in the final weeks of six months' intensive training to make them police officers. As the gym class began I could not help but be impressed by their fitness level as they went through an amazing range of exercises, most of which I attempted gently. One thing did puzzle me. Why, if these recruits were so fit when they left college, did a lot of police officers I had seen in America so far look as if they had been training in Dunkin' Donuts rather than the gym? It appeared that after the initial training period the new officers were left to do their job without any more regular exercise and the very real pressures of being a Miami cop did seem to cause a bit of plumpness here and there. Anyway, they were all in shape now and I was feeling pretty sore by the time we got to the weapon self-defence section of the class. One of the instructors taught me to go forward with arm outstretched ready to twist the weapon away from the assailant. I had to disarm another of the instructors, a tiny man who looked exactly like Joe Pesci in *GoodFellas.* I did what I was told, wrested the gun from Pesci's grip and took control of the situation, but I did wonder about the ease with which I managed this process. It struck me that in a real situation Pesci might struggle a bit more or pull the trigger a bit earlier. Then I was told that if you've not been shot in the first thirty seconds or so, you've got a 90 per cent chance of disarming your attacker. I sincerely hoped that I would never have the opportunity to prove this theory. The class ended with a spontaneous presentation to me of the official class cap and it was accompanied, as every trainee activity seemed to be, with a lot of orchestrated shouting of their group number and motto. 'BLE . . . 179 . . . United in spirit and mind,' they all barked at me as I walked, or to be more accurate limped, back to my place. Apparently I was now fit enough to learn how to do some real police work.

Just about the single most dangerous thing a police officer can do is something called the felony stop. That's when a known armed criminal is chased in his car, stopped and brought to justice by police officers. Instructor Dwyer took me out to the college driving range to teach me how to handle one. I was introduced to Officer Bulloch who would ride with me in one of two police cars chasing a bad guy with our sirens blaring and our lights flashing. I realised that in effect I was about to star in a police movie and I began quietly practising the dialogue I thought I might need as we waited for the signal to begin the pursuit. Somehow, 'You're nicked, my son,' did not sound convincing in these circumstances so I guessed that I would have to improvise. The signal was given, the chase was on and we had to drive right up behind the criminal's car to force him to stop. Then Instructor Dwyer talked me through the felony stop procedure. In one hand I held a bright red replica gun and in the other I had a microphone attached to a loudspeaker mounted on the police car. My task was to get the crook out of the car, convince him to dispose of his weapon, and direct him to take up a harmless position which would allow him to be safely arrested, all just by chatting to him.

And so began a bizarre square dance with each action being precisely described by me and acted out by the crook. The sequence was that he had to drop his keys out of the window, climb out of the car, step back towards me with his hands on his head, shuffle to the side to place him directly in front of our car, then get down so that we could arrest him. I bellowed exactly the words I was told to use through the microphone and we made what I felt confident must have been a textbook arrest. Instructor Dwyer was not so convinced. Apparently I had badly blotted my copybook with my use of the word 'sorry' during the incident when I had inadvertently given a wrong instruction and apologised to the crook. In America, I was told in no uncertain terms, it was not the done thing to say sorry to potentially dangerous criminals and I was also assured that stop-at-nothing desperadoes did not need to be thanked for responding promptly to instructions at any stage by officers arresting them. Otherwise, the instructor said, I had done well and had kicked felon ass, as they liked to say rather ungrammatically in this neck of the woods.

I had not enjoyed holding even a replica gun during the exercise but in America, and especially in Florida where gun controls were incredibly casual, no police work could be contemplated without carrying a weapon. That might have been the chill reality of the job I was learning to do but at the same time I did have to admit that on image Miami police work had got *The Bill* well beaten. Everything was so much more glamorous, from the cars to the uniforms. It was easy to forget that I was about to experience the real thing and not a movie where the director could shout 'Cut' if the action got a little out of hand. The Police Department had obviously predicted that I might be a little concerned about the prospect of walking the mean streets so they had seconded a media relations officer to set my mind at rest. Sergeant Ed Munn looked like the kind of good detective in a crime movie who gets very close to cracking the case, then is betrayed by the corrupt cop, shot by the baddies, and whose death is avenged by the real hero of the film. He had a calm, reassuring manner and talked proudly of how the Department had tackled the major problem of crime against tourists. Extra officers had been recruited and there had been a concentrated effort to catch the crooks who were preying on newly arrived tourists in their hire cars. Large rewards were placed on the heads of the ringleaders and gradually they were all caught as their families and former friends decided to cash in on their inside information.

Sergeant Munn knew that we British had a fairly grim view of the crime statistics in Miami but was at considerable pains to say we had it all out of proportion and told me a story to illustrate the point. A British television crew had recently come out to Miami to film with the Police Homicide Unit and were horrified to discover that the unit did not seem very busy. The producer was furious because he had been under the impression that there would be at least a murder a day. Sergeant Munn had been happy to tell the bloodthirsty producer that the police would not be able to provide anything like the rate he needed for his film. So life is apparently a lot safer now for residents and visitors in Miami but I have to say that precisely at the time Sergeant Munn was giving me the good news, the Dade County Police Department was dealing with two separate and horrific crimes. One was the murder of a young Bahamian child whose parents were the chief suspects and the other was the disappearance of a well-to-do local woman and her husband. It soon turned out that he had murdered her and then taken his own life in a motel room. Not even the cleverest media relations man could talk his way round those terrible stories. The reality for me was that I was about to put my life on the line as a serving police officer and if I had been signing up for life I would have been making that commitment for $25,000 a year plus health insurance, retirement benefits, and the right to take my police car home at night. Not the best deal I have been offered.

Sergeant Munn thought it would be a good idea for me to get a kind of overview of police work before hitting the beat so he asked me to report to Opa-Locka Airport at eight the next morning. I was intrigued by the weird name of the place so I did some investigation. Opa-Locka was a little city on the north-west side of Miami created in the real estate boom of the 1920s by a developer who took *The Arabian Nights* as his inspiration and gave all the buildings Moorish domes and minarets. The place has fallen on hard times and is pretty run down these days but you can still drive down Ali Baba Street.

The airport itself had a bit of fame because it was from there that Amelia Earhart took off in 1937 on her ill-fated trip round the world. Now it was a civil aviation centre and the base for the Metro Dade Police Aviation Unit. I was going to get a *real* overview sitting in the front of a police Jet Ranger helicopter on patrol in the skies above Miami. I was issued with a chocolate-brown flying suit and with my Ray-Bans on I started to feel very *Top Gun*. As they say, I felt the need, the need for speed. Unfortunately my pilot was not Tom Cruise. Bob Owen was a quiet man in his forties who had flown jets for Braniff Airlines, then come to this unit twelve years ago. He embodied the word laconic and as we took off I realised that I should not expect much in the way of flowery descriptions from this man. It was a disappointing Miami day because the cloud was down and rain was being forecast which meant that the view was not as good as it could have been but I still enjoyed seeing the shape of the city I was going to be policing. We flew over the area for around an hour and precisely nothing happened. Nobody asked us to follow any baddies or rescue anyone in distress so eventually we landed to face the greater challenge of deciding what to have for lunch. I was sure things would be more eventful on the ground.

I was told to report for duty the next day at the strangely named Haulover Park, North Miami Beach. It appeared that I was to be pounding the beach rather than the beat and I could have chosen worse places to begin my career as a law enforcement officer. Haulover Park was the greenest chunk of the Miami Beach area and was one of the best beaches in town. The first thing I noticed when I got to the small Haulover Park Police hut was that here, unlike every other inch of Miami shoreline, the developers seemed to have been kept at bay because a long stretch of the beach had no hotels or condominiums overlooking it. Just grassy dunes, trees and fresh air and it looked fantastic. The wind was blowing hard off the Atlantic. But it still felt warm and the sea was an incredible turquoise colour. I could get used to this. I had been issued with my beach detail uniform which was a white T-shirt with the Metro Dade County Police badge, extremely tight beige shorts, short white socks and boots. Before the addition of a belt with radio and other bits and pieces I looked more like a tourist than a cop, but perhaps that was the intention. *Dixon of Dock Green* this was not.

My partners for the day were straight out of central casting. Sergeant Tom Buchanan was six foot three, boyish-looking with floppy sandy-coloured hair and shorts that seemed to me to be illegally tight. He wore wraparound shades which never left his sculpted cheekbones, spoke with a lazy drawl and when he grinned the sun flashed off his perfect teeth. I asked about his obvious Caledonian roots and he told me that his family were indeed Scottish, coming from near to the border with Ireland. I guessed then that geography was not Sergeant Buchanan's strong points, but with freckles like his who needed O Levels?

Officer Kurt Brauty was very much the opposite of his partner being a five foot six squat, bald guy with a big black moustache. He was the more talkative of the two and admitted straight away that working the beach was a great job which he had been very happy to do for four years but he was leaving soon to work on a dangerous undercover unit. I noticed that he stopped smiling when he talked about his new posting.

I helped the two officers check the equipment they used for their patrols and little of it would qualify for standard police use. They did their main patrolling by foot or on red Kawasaki four-wheel drive all-terrain vehicles. I was delighted to see the little chubby wheeled quad bikes because we had one back home in England for zapping around our farm and carrying food and hay out to the pigs and sheep. I considered myself a bit of an expert on it. They also had white mountain bikes and it gave me a warm glow of patriotic pleasure to see that one of the bikes was a Raleigh, although it didn't look very much like the one my brother had when he was eleven. I also noticed a couple of Yamaha Jet Skis in official police colours in the back of the garage. Not many of those in the West Midlands Constabulary car park.

Today it was the ATVs which Sergeant Buchanan picked out for us and after a quick familiarisation with the controls I putt-putted off behind him. It's hard to retain dignity as a guardian of law and order when you are sitting astride what looks very like an oversized Tonka toy. Our patrol started down at the Newport fishing pier which stretched several hundred yards out into the crashing surf, and was surrounded by pelicans wheeling lazily on the air currents and occasionally swooping down into the water to grab a fish with their enormous beaks. They seemed to be having much more success than the humans fishing off the pier but none of the fishermen looked as if they minded too much. The calendar may have said February but it looked more like high summer on a Mediterranean beach to me as Tom (we had got a bit more informal by now) and I picked our way carefully through the oiled and bronzed bodies littering the sand. The task of the beach patrol was to maintain high visibility and to be on hand for any emergencies. Beaches do tend to be places where accidents are waiting to happen and the ocean is especially dangerous at Miami Beach because of huge sandbars just off the coast that cause treacherous rip currents capable of sucking even the strongest swimmer out to sea. In fact, Tom told me that a tourist had been drowned south of this beach just yesterday. I breathed a sigh of relief when he told me that as a policeperson I would not be expected to dive in to save anyone because there were plenty of hunky lifeguards lounging around in their *Baywatch*-style huts to do that job. Tom and I cruised the beach in the nicest possible way for a while and the closest we came to an incident was when I drove over someone's shoes. Luckily for all of us, the person concerned was not wearing them at the time.

America may be the Land of the Free but it has quite a lot of rules around to keep those Free people in order. I was driving across a stretch of American beach which looked exactly like a chunk of the Costa del Sol except for one tiny detail. There was not a naked breast in sight. I drove a mile through thousands of scantily clad sun worshippers and the journey was totally nipple-free for the simple reason that American women are not allowed to go topless on their beaches. I stopped for a second to check the logic of this: Florida rules permitted you to buy with the minimum of fuss a gun capable of killing people but the same rule book prohibited you from taking your top off on the beach. Tom shocked me out of my philosophical torment by announcing that we were about to head for the Nudist Beach. Apparently a few hundred yards south of the fishing pier, nudists had raised two fingers (at least I hope it was fingers) to the authorities and created a marked area where they could sunbathe as nature intended. The same authorities who banned topless sunbathing apparently turned a blind eye to what they were doing but, this being America, could not bring themselves to call the area a 'Nudist' beach. Instead I saw from the signs that we were approaching a 'Clothing Optional' beach and as we got closer I noticed that it also seemed to be a 'Women Optional' beach because there were not many gals around that I could see. Miami is a very gay town and much of the success of the city's cultural rebirth has been due to the efforts of the powerful gay community. It was the colonisation of the dilapidated South Beach area by gay people in the early Eighties which resulted in the renovation of the Art Deco architectural treasures there. I squinted into the dazzling sun to catch my first glimpse of a total sunbather and I spotted a man with his back to me striding purposefully along the edge of the surf. Then I realised to my disappointment that he was wearing trunks with a stripe down the middle and then I realised that was no stripe. I nearly crashed into a waste bin.

As a police officer I knew that I had the powers of arrest and in one or two cases I was very tempted to use them as we drove this section of beach which for some reason didn't remind me of Weston-super-Mare. I felt like a bit of a voyeur as we picked our way very carefully through the sunbathers but all of them were totally relaxed and seemed untroubled by our presence. Tom had warned me that there were often arrests on the Nudist Beach for 'Lewd Behaviour' but the lewdest thing I could see was a bit of suncream application amongst consenting adults. I did nearly stall my ATV when one man crossed in front of me and almost caused a partial eclipse of the sun. Take it from someone who has worked on the Genito-Urinary Ward at the Queen Elizabeth Hospital in Birmingham that this was an exceptional young man. Tom noticed my reaction and told me about a well-known character on the beach who was affectionately known as 'Tripod'. Apparently he was disappointed for some reason that socks came in pairs rather than threes. We carried on through the acres of exposed flesh and I tried hard to concentrate on steering straight. I almost lost it when a guy approached me from a distance. I had to hope that he was naked because if he wasn't, that was a very strange bag he was carrying. I realised that a good cop needs to know his or her local community well, but this was ridiculous.

The next day Tom decided that I could fly solo after spending a little more time with him first. This time we left the ATVs in the garage and walked along the beach. Tom took the liberty of telling me how impressed he had been by my abilities on the ATV but before I could bask in the glory of my driving skills he did point out that he was not quite so enamoured with my walking. Apparently I didn't walk enough like a cop and he thought it vital that he teach me how to do the law enforcement stroll. I had to stand straighter, move slower and hold my hands out from my sides at all times so they were ready to grab my weapon. Which, in my case, was a paper hankie. His instructions worked and I began to feel more like Mr John Wayne than Mrs

Overall as I strode alongside him. The continued complete lack of incident on the beach gave me the chance to talk to Tom who was getting much warmer towards me than he had been the day before. He must have been older than he looked because he had been in the police for sixteen years and it had taken him twelve of those years to get to the detail he wanted on the beach. He laughed when I told him that not much seemed to happen there and calmly recounted the story of a sniper who had tried to shoot him last year on patrol. He also talked about the regular summer visits to the beach by huge gatherings of kids from the notorious Liberty City area which always ended up in violence and gunfights. Also every day he had to face the problem of beach theft, there was the permanent danger of the ocean, and it was his responsibility to control the Lewdness back on Plonker Beach. Tom laughed that none of those duties really scared him but admitted that he was genuinely worried about his regular partner Kurt whom I had met earlier. He felt that Kurt's new job in an undercover team working the drugs world was suicidally dangerous and he was crazy to be giving up the beach for it. Talking about violent criminals who murdered anyone who got in their way without the slightest compunction kind of got this policing job in perspective for me. I knew where I would choose if I was a Metro Dade County Police officer and sand would definitely be involved.

Tom was now convinced that I had done well enough in my duties to be allowed to walk the beach on my own but with him in close radio attendance at all times. It was another perfect Florida day with the temperature in the low eighties, a strong sea breeze, and the sun blasting out its rays from a cloudless sky. I made sure I was covered in suncream before I went out on patrol because the most dangerous thing I had faced in the last couple of beach days was nasty sunburn on my neck. Not even the strongest bullet-proof vest could save me from that. Luckily, they sold good old Calamine lotion over here if the worst came to the worst but it was better to take precautions. The beach was packed with families but I noticed that not many people were braving the sea. There had been a lot in the local papers and on television about tragedies caused by the rip currents and the lifeguards were flying warning flags saying the currents were a danger. Only a few people were playing the macho card and even they were not venturing out far. So, feeling rather self-conscious and desperately trying to control my posture, I set off down the beach. Very little happened except that I had to try to answer life and death questions like 'Can you swim beside that pier?' and 'Who are that film crew shooting?' The answers were: no, because the pier was for fishing only; and me, have you got a problem with that?

Then when I got near to the Newport pier again on my route back a young girl beckoned me over and told me that she had seen a suspicious-looking guy hanging around on the beach looking at her and other women. She had watched him behave weirdly for a while, then seen him head off towards a block of apartments a short distance away. A real incident, real police work and I quickly radioed Tom with shaking fingers. He could not have been more laconic as he agreed to send some officers to check it out but he did end by telling me that I had done a good job. I was in business and was now bursting for an arrest. I began to wonder if there were any local by-laws concerning offensive swimwear.

Tom called on the radio to order me to patrol south of the pier and that could mean only one thing. I was going to have to walk through the Nudist Beach without so much as a truncheon to protect me. I needn't have worried because in the end I thought I looked pretty cool as I walked my police walk in amongst all the deeply tanned boys. My biggest challenge was to answer questions from stark naked males without ever once lowering my gaze. Tom had told me to watch out for a real character who described himself as the Mayor of the Nudist Beach. It was not difficult to find him because he always sat at the same point and flew a flag from his sun lounger. The incredibly tanned Mayor was probably in his sixties. He was going through a T'ai Chi stretching routine and I tried to match his movements as we chatted. He turned out to be the oldest ex-hippy in town and we got on like a house on fire. Within five minutes he was giving me a fantastic neck massage and trying to locate my aura. I warned him that I could probably arrest him for that but he didn't seem to mind. We talked for a while, I the female police officer and he the bald elderly man with no clothes on, and not surprisingly the subject came round to clothes and their place in society. The Mayor was passionate in his belief that getting naked made people better human beings and suggested that many more people should try it. I was going to tell him about the potential problems of getting naked on Skegness Beach with a Force Eight blowing but I decided it wasn't worth the effort. I took my leave of the Mayor and carried on along the beach to finish my patrol, thinking as I did that it was a very good idea in the interests of public relations that officers were asked not to assume the uniform of the beach when they worked on it. Where on earth would I have kept my notebook?

Tom had another treat in store for me when I got back to base because he decided that I was now ready to take on waterway patrol duties. We climbed into a police pick-up truck and drove west through the park to the narrow strip of water between North Miami Beach and the mainland. This was the Intra-Coastal Waterway and it came under the jurisdiction of the Beach Police. I helped Tom unload one of the Jet Skis I had seen back in the garage and had to admit to him that I might have been an expert on the ATV but could not make the same claim for this craft. Apparently there was no problem because I would be riding pillion. No amount of police crests and badges could disguise the fact it was straight out of a Club Med brochure and after all my training and experience I rather felt that riding it was beneath me. A short twenty minutes later I was undergoing one of the most frightening experiences of my life. Facing backwards on the Jet Ski, holding onto the handrails by my fingertips, and rocketing over the water at what seemed like 250 miles an hour. All I could see was an enormous jet of water which shot about twenty feet in the air from near my feet and some Florida scenery blurring behind it. I summoned up all my physical strength and reserves of courage and tried to take myself in hand. I managed in the best way I could in the circumstances. I opened my mouth and screamed 'Help!'

Tom did hear me eventually and we returned to base before there was any call-out to chase some stolen speedboat or something. I would seriously have considered the ejector seat option if that had happened. And so ended my time as Metro Dade County Police officer. Putting that Jet Ski experience to one side I had enjoyed most of the time I had spent learning and doing the job but I realised that I had been kept well away from the real dangers that most of the police officers face every day in Miami. No amount of civic redecoration can hide the fact that Miami is a town where crime flourishes and guns are easier to come by than almost anywhere else in the States. Thank goodness there were men and women prepared to put their lives on the line but don't think about including me in that number. I'm a bit of a coward and I don't mind admitting it. What I needed to find now was a job which had no risk attached to it at all. . . .

6

We're Looking for a Pig, Officer

Pesky Critters Animal Catchers

*M*iami is a dramatic place, a heady mix of colours, characters and substances, some of them exotic, many of them wild. It is also, I was about to discover, home to an astonishing number of animals, many of them exotic, some of them very wild indeed. Forget North America when you reach the tip of Southern Florida and prepare yourself for the tropics. When they said it was a jungle out there in Miami it didn't occur to me that they were being literal. The sub-tropical conditions in the deepest of the deep American South make the State of Florida a breeding place for some of the most extraordinary creatures on earth and if it wasn't for all those Miami nightclubs to keep them in I really don't think the streets would be safe to walk. However, there is not such an enlightened policy when it comes to animals and the city and state have a problem dealing with genuine wildlife invading the human domain. Florida is crawling with living things all the way from the ant to the mighty alligator and often these creatures want to enjoy parts of their territory which man has decided to call his own. Combined with these indigenous locals, Florida is also bristling with a bizarre collection of alien beings, all of whom I empathise with heavily, in the form of pets of every size, type, and nationality which residents have acquired over the years. Many of these pets decide to find out more about their new home State and set off to go walkabout into other people's properties and lives. At one time, if a Florida resident discovered one of these uninvited animal guests on their property the State would send someone around to sort things out. However, in the early 1980s the politicians decided that they could only afford to handle problems caused by small rather than large pests. Cockroaches they would still help with but if you had a rare Florida panther sharpening his claws on your gazebo you were very much on your own, mate.

It was then that a saviour was delivered to the beleaguered people of Florida. Todd Hardwick was a local teenager who had discovered his vocation in life at a tender age when he captured his first possum. He realised then that he was born to trap animals, always humanely and never for sport, and he began teaching himself the techniques to take on any of Florida's lengthy roster of potential escapees. He set up his company in 1981 and began, part-time at first, keeping the backyards of Florida safe for people to empty trash cans in without fear of attack from some furry raider. By 1985 he was full time and the undisputed market leader, referred to by all the emergency services and on permanent twenty-four-hour call. Hardwick had created an empire in nuisance wildlife control and his company name spelled out the scale and grandeur of his vision. Today, Saturday 22nd February, which also happened to be my birthday, I was to report for duty with Pesky Critters.

I set off before 8 a.m. towards the company's headquarters in Homestead, a suburban expanse about twenty miles south of downtown Miami. It looked like a fairly unremarkable place with the usual collection of familiar franchises and unimaginative architecture ranged along the South Dixie Highway but a few years before this ordinary neighbourhood had been at the centre of one of the biggest American news stories of the century. Just before dawn on 24th August 1992 Hurricane Andrew arrived in South Florida, and Homestead and the surrounding areas took a direct hit. Andrew turned out to be a Category Five hurricane which is so rare that only one or two that severe occur in a hundred years and it created America's worst ever natural disaster. The State was left with a bill for $20 billion of damage and over 150,000 were made homeless. Hurricane Andrew turned Homestead into a war zone and even five years on from those dark days I noticed that the locals liked to turn the subject of any conversation round to Andrew. I suppose we have generations in Britain who remember the Second World War clearly and don't believe it should be forgotten so the Homesteaders have every right to keep their personal natural Blitz memories at the forefront of their minds.

I have to admit that foremost in my mind at that moment were thoughts of my new employment. I had been given a copy of a Pesky Critters brochure and on it I saw that they used the slogan 'Who ya gonna call?' which I am pretty sure I remember being used somewhere else. There was also a list of ten clues which indicated you needed the company's service. A few items tickled me:

Your neatly manicured lawn looks like a public chip and putt course.

Your fish pond is fished out.

It sounds like the midnight bowling league is competing in your attic.

The pride and joy of your backyard aviary has mysteriously flown the coop . . . and left behind all of its feathers.

The rest of the document explained my job specifications eloquently: 'Pesky Critters specializes in capturing wild and exotic animals alive and unharmed. We utilize cage traps for the capture of urban wildlife such as raccoons, opossums, foxes, bobcats, etc. Difficult animal captures and high risk situations are safely managed with the use of state of the art equipment ranging from tranquillizer rifles to custom designed gear.' There were also some photographs which rather worryingly concentrated on lengthy snakes and ferocious alligators. I was hoping to focus more on the cuddly end of the evolutionary scale as a beginner. Don't get me wrong, I love animals and we have an interesting collection of our own at home but I've always had doubts about getting close to ones which liked to eat me. Actually, what scares me the most was something not featured in the brochure and something I was praying would not feature in my duties. I was prepared to go face to face with raccoons, opossums, foxes, even alligators, as long as I never had to touch a spider. Big, small, hairy, poisonous, harmless, whatever. Show me an eight-leg arachnid and I'll show you a three-minute mile.

The world headquarters of Pesky Critters was in the middle of one of those American roads which seem to go on in a straight line for ever. This was Miami's outer suburbia and all I could see were acres of orchards dotted with neat bungalows. There was no clue as I pulled into the drive that the neat yellow bungalow which served as the nerve centre for the Pesky Critters operation was anything special other than the fact there was a model deer standing in the front yard and quite the fiercest smelling rubbish bins I have ever had the misfortune to sniff, waiting to be collected outside the gate. That and the occasional scream of an animal or bird which sounded as if it was not of the small, domestic or cuddly categories. Todd Hardwick came out of the house to meet me. He was a slim, thin-faced, thirty-something man with receding blond hair and the kind of tight jeans that got me worrying about blood supply to his lower extremities. However, he seemed to be coping and began to introduce me to my new working environment. What became instantly clear was that Pesky Critters was not a large operation despite its success. Pesky Critters was Todd Hardwick and that was it. I did glean from him that there was a lady in his life called Jill but she was conspicuous by her absence. It turned out that she was in the house but she showed no signs of wanting to come out to meet her partner's new work-mate. Later on a bizarre trip to the loo I did overhear a conversation between Todd and Jill which suggested to me that she was not 100 per cent behind the idea of me being there along with a film crew. She used a variety of adjectives to describe me and the situation and they were all considerably stronger than 'pesky'. So, Todd could tame a gator but not a girl. Interesting. The trip to the Ladies was bizarre, by the way, because the loo sat in the middle of a giant model of a shark's mouth. The symbolism was lost on me.

The sound of terrible screaming and moaning filled the air as we got closer to the house and before I could ask what on earth was going on Todd had shown me the answer. Behind the bungalow there was a long expanse of open land leading down to an orchard area with coconut and mango trees. The noise was coming from the top half of his property which was littered with cages and pens of all shapes and sizes housing a menagerie of wildlife. Todd captured animals for a living and it turned out that he personally kept lots of his captives in a private zoo with over

150 residents. The noises came from a pair of beautiful Amazonian macaws which were competing with each other in a 'who's got the loudest screech' competition. There was also a stunning white parakeet whose conversation started and stopped with the word 'hello'. It occurred to me that it had probably not been taught by Jill.

I was learning fast that Todd had a much more extensive vocabulary than his partner and was adept at using it. He was at considerable pains to tell me that the job I was about to do was fraught with danger and I detected a worrying glint in his pale blue eyes when he talked about the damage many of these animals could wreak on a small English body such as mine. He did admit that he had been in a 'hospitalisation situation' only twice in his animal handling career and it had not been panthers or alligators which put him there. The two fierce creatures which sent him to ER were actually a smelly but small skunk and a powerful but petite possum. The injuries inflicted were not even particularly spectacular. In fact the hospital visits came about because Todd got a touch of infection after each incident. Hardly *Jaws 2*. Todd looked quite downcast as he relayed his medical misfortunes and I gradually realised that he was actually craving a real injury. It was then I had my first real doubts about volunteering to go into hand to paw combat action with a man like this. Todd obviously sensed a shift in my attitude and at that point produced a pair of leather gauntlets. They were, he proudly declared, constructed of Kevlar, the substance used to make bullet-proof vests. As far as I knew, we would be meeting no animals which carried guns but I did feel more relaxed as I slipped on the rather stylish brown and yellow hand protectors. Todd gave another of his somewhat chilling smiles as he described the quality of the gauntlets, 'They will stop bullets so no critters' teeth can penetrate them.' Suddenly he grabbed my gloved hand and began twisting it hard from side to side. 'But they can't stop critters a-crunchin' and a-crushin' you!' Thank you *very* much, Todd.

Todd decided that I should face a sort of initiation test to prepare me for the rigours ahead. The way he had been talking I fully expected to have to go alone into a cage to manually extract a rotten tooth from a crazed mountain lion but he had another idea. He brought one of those little plastic pet carrier boxes you take your kitten to the vet in and asked me to stick in my hand and bring out the contents. Working on the principle that I would be considerably bigger than whatever I found there I plunged in a Kevlar-clad hand and forearm and rummaged around in the straw. After a few minutes I felt a small ball which I lifted out to reveal a cute little hedgehog that made no attempt to a-crunch or a-crush me. This was Freddy the African hedgehog, an escaped pet who now lived in the Hardwick zoo and seemed a very nice little thing. I had passed the test and was now deemed brave enough to face the worst Miami could throw at me. We settled down to wait for a call. While we sat around Todd told me a bit more about the economics of wildlife control. He had a standard call-out fee of $75 for any animal, big or small, and it was only payable if the creature was caught. Alligators were actually free because they were the one animal the State of Florida would still pay to have captured. It was felt that it would be unfair for anyone to be stuck with an unwanted gator around the house because they happened to be short of money at that time.

The first call happened around lunchtime and so Todd and I climbed into his brand-new Dodge pick-up truck and headed off to a house a couple of miles away to sort out a problem with a rat-like creature with big teeth which had taken temporary residence in the garage. Todd guessed that it was probably a possum and took the trouble to let me know that the opossum is the only indigenous marsupial in the United States and it happens to possess the greatest number of teeth of any creature in the country. 'Like razors,' he muttered as we headed towards the stricken family laden with all the gear necessary for wildlife control. We had long catchpoles, nets, cages, snake tongs, and even tranquilliser guns. Tranquilliser for me or the animals? 'Those possums are unpredictable and lightning fast,' Todd warned me as we turned into the drive of another yellow low-slung bungalow almost invisible in dense jungle-like greenery.

The man of the house came out to meet us. Russ Calhoun was a very tall man, probably around six feet five, in his mid-fifties and proudly sporting a shaggy beard and a long grey pigtail. It did strike me that if a man of his size and stature was calling us out to get rid of a possum then maybe these furry creatures were less fun than I had first thought. Russ led us to his huge garage where the beast was holed up behind the water heater. I could just see the tip of a cuddly nose and was commenting on how sweet he looked when Todd hit me with more of the B movie-type dialogue he favoured to keep me scared. 'He looks cute now but that will change real quick and he'll bite you and put a hurtin' on you.' Everything did happen real quick after that. Todd poked at the possum who started hissing menacingly and then decided to come out from the safety of the heater and straight into our trap. Todd somehow lost his glove in the confusion and started screaming at me to pick up a now very vexed beast. I went to grab the little blighter up by the tail and get him into the cage. By now I had realised sweetness was not a major possum quality and I panicked that he would curl up and start biting my hand.

Todd assured me that everything would be fine so I grabbed the toothy mammal by the point furthest away from his dental work and chucked him into the wire cage we had brought. At first the little bugger grabbed the mesh of the cage and anchored himself alarmingly near the lid but eventually gravity took him down to a safe position, the cage could be locked and I could breathe again. My heart was pumping fiercely but I walked out of that garage a little taller than when I went in.

The drama of the last few moments quickly paled as I chatted to the Calhouns and talk soon got round to the number one Homestead topic. Russ described vividly what it had been like in 1992 when the eye of Hurricane Andrew passed over the house we were standing beside. He had built the place himself and had sensibly included a cupola device on the roof which allowed the enormous pressures generated by the hurricane to be dispelled without leaving the house looking like a convertible. He talked laconically about the effects of the 200 miles per hour winds which wiped out every tree and most buildings around them in a thirty-mile-wide swathe of destruction. He remembered the actual eye passing directly over the house and for ten minutes there was an eerie calm. That is, Russ pointed out, if you think that 100 miles per hour gales qualify as eerie calm. It was as if they were in the middle of a giant doughnut with a four-mile hole of clear skies above and a circle of ferocious blackness around them. Russ, with that extreme understatement favoured by American pilots and astronauts, told me that it had 'not been a fun experience'.

Day Two of my Pesky Critters experience dawned bright and warm again. It was hard to believe that this was February and we were actually facing the rigours of a Florida winter. It was a chilly 75 degrees Fahrenheit (the Americans still like their temperatures in old money) as I arrived at Critters Central, and later that day it would reach a brisk 85 degrees in the shade. Lucky I had brought my thermals. Our first job of the day was a rather tame affair which involved us picking up two placid raccoons which climbed into cages of their own accord and travelled uncomplainingly back to Todd's zoo where they were delighted to meet lots of fellow raccoons, many of whom they probably knew. I was just beginning to get a little cocky about this job when Todd's mobile rang. I heard him say the words, 'How big,' 'Don't move,' and 'Snake,' and realised that the easy jobs were probably over for the day. When he began to discuss the possibility with the caller that the family cat may have become lunch for this unwelcome visitor beads of sweat began to form on my forehead.

Todd had been doing this job a long time and knew all about snakes and how humans reacted to them. He was completely dismissive of any length estimate given to him by panicky callers because he cynically believed that people always massively exaggerated the size of the snake they had sighted so that he would come in a hurry to help them out. My personal view was that any snake over the size of a common garden worm qualifies as enormous. This caller had said he had seen the snake outside his house under the family car and the reptile had stretched from the front to the rear axles. That meant it could be eight feet long and that was a monster in my book. As usual, Todd began reeling off as many gory facts as he had in that strange head of his. He was confident that it would not be a venomous snake we were tackling because they were rare in this part of the world. In fact, South Florida could only boast four venomous snakes: the Eastern diamond-backed rattlesnake, the pygmy rattlesnake, the cottonmouth water moccasin, and the coral snake. The cottonmouth water one sounded more like a new kind of Clarks shoe than an angel of death but Todd did not look like a man talking footwear.

The Knox family lived about eight or nine miles away in a very ordinary suburban road. Other than the fact there was a giant snake rampaging through the neighbourhood and there was an American flag flying rather limply from a pole on the front porch, we could almost have been pulling up in Acacia Avenue, Basingstoke. Todd went into the house to speak to the owner while I gathered up a collection of the tools we might need for the job. There was no sign of a Chieftain tank in the back of the truck. So, I was going into life-threatening action clutching a pair of snake tongs which looked only a couple of degrees up from the tongs we used to plop sugar lumps in cups of tea, and wearing my trusty Kevlar gloves. Perfect.

We quickly worked out that the snake was no longer under the car and had probably slithered into the backyard. Mr Knox revealed these facts from deep within the safety of his sitting room. He and the rest of the Knox family had decided that they were not coming out until Hissing Sid was history. Todd was now in full flow and he virtually dragged me into a trim backyard with a lawn of Bermuda grass, some brightly coloured kids' toys scattered around, and a large white wooden shed. When I saw the shed I knew immediately that this snake would have followed the basic rule of movie scripts and headed for the most claustrophobic and scary location available. I was right. We were tracking a snake with an eye for dramatic tension and minutes later I was nervously peering around in the semi-darkness of the junk-filled shed. Todd mentioned the chilling fact that if the snake was half as big as it was reputed to be, finding it in this confined space would be easy. He then began poking at rubbish in the roof while I moved gingerly around seeing giant snakes behind every box and rolled-up carpet on the dusty floor. I was petrified that Todd's lunges at the ceiling would bring the snake crashing down on us and my heart rate was in overdrive. Todd moved up to the far end of the shed and I felt a bit safer concentrating on the other end which was stacked with the usual mess of carpet rolls, tarpaulins and boxes that seem to be in every shed. Suddenly I saw something move. Actually, that's wrong. Suddenly I saw everything move because all the carpet rolls and junk shifted towards me menacingly. As I stared in disbelief I caught a glimpse of a bit of what we were looking for in the middle of the clutter. It was definitely a snake but I had never seen one quite like this before. The coil I was looking at must have been the thickness of a child's waist and it took a second or two before I could collect myself enough to stammer out the news.

Todd got very excited when he heard my quavering revelation and leaped over to where I pointed. I had no idea what size this thing was but as my eyes got used to the gloom I saw that the head which had been facing me seemed a considerable distance away from the other end. Todd screamed at me to hold down the head while he located the rest of the snake and without thinking I attempted to perform my first snake head lock. As I put my hands on the snake's neck two thoughts flashed through my mind. First, a snake doesn't have a neck, it's all neck, and second, wouldn't I hurt the poor snake if I got too rough? As my hands gripped tighter the snake casually flicked them off with a twist of its head. I think I might have been flattering myself a little about being a serious contender in this match. Todd was in his element now with a full-blown exotic animal danger situation in progress. He shouted to me, and he was just eight inches away from my right ear at the time, that if the snake anchored its tail somewhere we would definitely never be able to shift him. I did think that maybe we would have to load the whole shed onto the back of a lorry and take it back to base. Then Todd grabbed the tail and we were winning again. I picked up a bit of snake and it felt incredibly smooth, warm and heavy, definitely not cold and slimy as people always think. I could feel the enormous muscular power in the coils as we attempted to drag this snake out of the confines of the shed. It took a long time to get all of it through the door and once it was lying on the grass outside I realised that this snake was extremely long and could crush me to death without batting an eyelid. And I had worried that I might hurt it! As I struggled painfully to help Todd lift it into a large pet container I breathlessly asked him if it was a boy or girl snake. 'It don't matter right now,' he said tersely.

We had just captured ourselves a genuine python which stretched to around sixteen feet and, according to Todd, weighed in at 120 pounds or so. That's nearly nine stones of snake, considerably more than I had ever planned dealing with in my life. Now that the python was safely under lock and key, I could find out a bit more about Monty, as I now felt safe in calling him. Monty was definitely a boy and I was interested to discover that boy snakes are extremely well-endowed creatures. More in the numbers department than size because they happen to be the proud possessors of two willies. You just never know when you are going to need a spare. Otherwise snakes have all the same bits inside as us, although arranged a bit differently. I was aware that pythons are constrictors so they go in for crushing their prey but Todd revealed that they also have an impressive set of teeth which can give a nasty bite. There are actually four rows of teeth on a python's upper jaw and two on the bottom, all curved inwards to help them hold things. How cruel of nature, two penises and no arms.

I felt completely exhausted after the physical and mental strain of capturing Monty and I was pleased to see that Todd looked as if he was also suffering. He suggested we call it a day and I was happy to agree. Once I had got my breath back I had time to think about the job we had just done and it did slightly concern me that my starring role as Indiana Jones had just earned the Pesky Critters organisation the princely sum of $37.50, half of the standard $75 fee Todd charged for the call-out. It did not seem anywhere near enough but I was too tired to complain. We put Monty on the back of the pick-up and headed back to base. We found out later that he was actually the pet of a twelve-year-old boy who lived in the next street to the Knox family and that his real name was Bart after the character in *The Simpsons.* Todd reunited the five-foot one-inch master with his sixteen-foot pet and warned him to take better care in the future. Bart promised that he would.

My next tour of duty at Pesky Critters was a pig of a day. The call came through early from a Mr Petrovic in the Princeton area complaining about a dark-coloured pig-like creature doing some uncommissioned landscaping in his back garden. We were on our way. At last I felt vaguely qualified for the job because back home in England we kept some pigs on our land and I fancied myself as a bit of an expert on the curly tail front. I was even able to suggest to Todd that the description of our mission target sounded suspiciously like a Vietnamese pot-bellied pig, because we had one of them at home in amongst our British normal-bellied variety. He agreed with my piggy prediction and I felt my exotic animal handling reputation moving into a new dimension.

It was mid-morning as we arrived at the Petrovic residence in yet another featureless suburban street. The temperature was beginning to climb into the high eighties and the humidity was heading over the 75 per cent mark. I'm not saying very little happened in that area but we did find a lights-flashing, siren-sounding police car stopped in the middle of the road outside the house. A stray pig was obviously a major incident in Princeton. As he approached the sweating police officer standing beside his squad car, Todd said, 'We're looking for a pig.' The irony of that line did not seem to register with either of them and the officer pointed over at the large house on his right and told us that it was round the back. We rushed round the side of the house and I prepared myself to witness a scene of devastation. If our highly strung British Vietnamese pot-bellied pig had been loose for a while in the back garden of the Petrovic house the immaculate lawn would have been destroyed. But this well-adjusted Florida Vietnamese pot-bellied pig was only interested in hanging out at the pool. There were no signs of damage anywhere to be seen and after a token struggle and a few piteous grunts he surrendered meekly to Todd's somewhat theatrical advances. Why we needed to have police cover for such a tame incident, I'll never know. Maybe the pig had a record.

My experience so far as a Pesky Critter person was already different from any other job I had done in my life but the next job we had to work on was downright weird. I had the strong feeling that I was taking part in an *X Files* show but in this episode Scully and Mulder were exchanging meaningful glances and saying to each other, 'This is just too far-fetched . . .' It all began with a call from a family in Cutler Ridge saying that there was some kind of animal running wild in their garden. It was a goat, just a kid, if you'll pardon the expression, and it was crashing around the large back garden of this house. It took quite a bit of time and energy from Todd and me to finally catch the goat because the poor thing was scared out of its wits and in no mood to be captured. What was weird was that I noticed as we got closer to the goat it seemed to be covered in scraps of paper. Eventually we got the panic-stricken animal cornered beside the swimming pool and only after Todd had spectacularly lunged straight into the deep end did we manage to subdue it. The bits of paper stuck all over its frantically panting body turned out to be dollar bills, probably twenty in all and mainly in ten-dollar denominations. Todd looked at this bizarre sight and said one word, 'Voodoo.'

Miami is a mix of influences from all over the world and its citizens have brought many cultures and beliefs to the United States. It may be the late Nineties for the civilised world but there are still people who believe in the power of voodoo. Todd described how parts of South Florida were littered with the signs of the cult of Santeria voodoo from the Caribbean. The goat we had just captured had been a short time away from becoming a living sacrifice to the God of Prosperity, slaughtered wearing dollar bills to please that idol. He must have escaped just seconds before becoming history and his successful bid for freedom meant there were now some very disenchanted voodoo believers having trouble paying their bills. Todd seemed to know a lot about this subject and described how he had found various animals sacrificed on railroad tracks to the God of Iron, and in water to the Goddess of Love. Strangely, believers also left birthday cakes and candles around these sacrifices. He said that there had been a recent Supreme Court judgement which allowed sacrifice as long as it was humanely done and, obviously, not involving a human. It seemed a bit of a contradiction in terms, humanely sacrificing a living being. For me, it seems pretty much impossible to sacrifice anything humanely. *In*humanely is surely the right word. Anyway, the goat had escaped a fate considerably worse than death and now he was going back to live at Pesky Critters Central with the lovely Jill. On second thoughts . . .

I had one day left to spend in Todd's world and I hoped it would be a quiet one. I realised that he was providing a genuine service to the people of Florida but I couldn't help but feel that some of his motives might be a bit misplaced. I'm sure he had been putting on a performance during the week for my sake but his obsession with the vicious side of some animals made me feel uneasy. Despite the fact he cared for literally hundreds of animals at his house, and cared for them very well, there was little sign of love or affection in Todd's dealings with animals. I'm no psychologist but I think what he enjoyed was the power he exerted over them. Maybe I should have had a chat with Jill on this subject. I am sure that she would have had some interesting thoughts. As we sat around Todd's bungalow listening to the animal orchestra tuning up in his garden I noticed that he had put up a sign on his fence which read 'Beware of the Dog'. I don't know how the Trades' Description Act works in the United States but a garden with over 150 animals in it, many of them dangerous, needed a more explicit notice, if you ask me. I had a nasty image of the postman being pursued by one of Todd's giant monitor lizards, screaming, 'What kind of dog is this?' Actually, because we were in America, the postman would be directing his screams at his attorney and Todd would probably soon be facing a $50 million lawsuit.

Everything went well on my last day until precisely twenty to five in the afternoon when Todd took a call on his mobile as we cruised along in the truck. I was getting used to him over-dramatising situations by this time but I did notice that he went a little pale under his Florida tan as he listened intently to the message. He asked just two questions, 'Where's he headed?' and 'How big is he?' before switching off the phone. It was a much grimmer Todd who explained that we had been called out to handle the kind of emergency he wasn't sure a greenhorn like me was ready for. Someone in the Howard neighbourhood had seen an alligator strolling the sidewalks and I think I was getting the message from Todd that this gator wasn't looking particularly happy. He told me that taking a gator out of water always makes for a dangerous animal and accordingly we would be tackling it with our catchpoles only. There would be no hand to hand combat with any crazed alligator which was obviously a little disappointing for me. Todd had a shopping list of alligator bad points including their vicious claws which can, as Todd put it, 'rip and shred', and the fact that their jaws can exert a pressure of over 3,000 pounds per square inch and that they do sometimes enjoy a human snack. The only positive factor we were looking at was that this gator was estimated at six to eight feet long which Todd rated as quite small and well within the capability of the two of us to subdue. He explained the techniques we would use to capture our gator. First we had to noose him with our catchpoles and then, at which point I started to find it difficult to breathe properly, one of us would have to sit on the gator's back and tape up his mouth. At this point Todd proudly flourished a roll of black insulating tape as if the sight of it alone would put my mind at rest. So, I was going to capture a ferocious reptile using only my brute strength and an item from a domestic toolkit. A terrible image of Jeremy Beadle suddenly floated into my mind. He was wearing a sparkly suit and was welcoming viewers to a brand-new television show. It was called *You've Been Maimed*.

I did know a couple of things about alligators. The difference between them and crocodiles is that gators like fresh water and crocs prefer salt. Also if a large low-slung reptile is approaching, you can quickly tell if you are about to be eaten by a crocodile or an alligator by looking closely at its mouth. If two teeth are protruding from the upper jaw when the mouth is closed you are about to say hello to Mr Crocodile. Todd told me that there were only two kinds of alligators in the world: American and Chinese. The oriental version lives in the Yangtse river and is very endangered whilst the American model inhabits the south-eastern section of the States and is doing fine. The huge numbers of farmed alligators in Florida mean that the wild gators are left alone and they are no longer under threat of extinction. Todd told me that anything over ten feet was big for gators in Florida these days but the American record was held by a Louisiana gator which measured nineteen feet two inches. That was back in the last century but there had been some eighteen-footers sighted in more recent times so I checked again with Todd about the length of the beast we were going to capture. He confirmed that this was a six-foot comparative tiddler. He also told me that this was not an unusual call-out for him because Miami did have a real alligator problem. The city's huge waterway and storm drain systems were all connected which allowed adventurous alligators to travel miles away from their territory to end up in the middle of suburbia.

The address we had been given was 151st Street off 71st Crescent, deep in the heart of suburbia, and the neighbourhood was as quiet and featureless as all the rest of the Miami outlands we had been working in. What struck me again as we pulled into a tree-lined cul de sac was the fact that we never saw any children playing anywhere we went. Every one of these suburban streets seemed deserted and devoid of the noisy kids and toys which would fill any British neighbourhood scene with life. Where were the Miami children? I suppose that the threat of a rampaging killer alligator might have an influence on the number of kiddiewinks playing on the road but it still seemed weird to me. Todd parked the pick-up and as we got out we could see a small knot of people gathered at the end of the cul de sac. They were moving towards us and after a while I realised there was actually a dark, scuttling shape in front of them. We had just discovered our alligator and it certainly did not look in the mood to be captured. Todd shouted at me to grab the catchpoles and follow him. The gator was moving remarkably quickly on its stubby little legs over the grass verge as Todd tried to head him off but the blighter made a dash for the gate to a backyard and as we followed we realised what he was up to. He was headed for the swimming pool and, using a body swerve that Stanley Matthews in his prime would have been proud of, he evaded Todd's despairing final lunge and slithered into the deep end. Now he was in his true environment and I don't know if it was the refracting effect of the water but he looked twice as big as he lay on the bottom of the pool. It looked as if the whole neighbourhood had turned out to see the excitement and we had quite a large audience as Todd and I poked at our prey with our catchpoles. The hot sun was very low now and long shadows rippled over the pool as we paced up and down the side. What was once a pleasant spot for a family to enjoy themselves had been transformed into a place filled with fear and terror. The monster was on the loose and only Todd and I stood between Miami and mayhem. But what was really scary was that I was now thinking in the same B-movie dialogue that Todd had been using with me all week.

It took about half an hour before Todd got his catchpole

noose round the gator's neck and managed to whip him onto the pool-side. Then everything went into fast forward. Todd screamed at me to hold the catchpole and keep the gator still while he got ready to sit on his back. The unhappy animal whipped his head and tail violently from side to side and I saw just how powerful it was. I had not really thought what kind of noise an alligator would make but I didn't expect the angry hissing sound which now echoed round the pool. Todd then told me to drop the pole and come forward to tape up his mouth. I hesitated for a second to work out if he meant the alligator's mouth or his own but I realised that I would need further instructions from Todd's lips so made my own selection. It's a strange feeling taking out a roll of tape and binding up a deadly alligator as if it was a vase you were sending to your Auntie Vi in Australia for Christmas. But that is exactly what I did and I got so involved in doing a good job that I even leaned forward to bite off the end of the tape when I was finished, forgetting the lethal jaws just inches below my face. All the while I was being scrutinised by one unblinking eye as the gator stared up at me darkly. One unblinking eye because I could not help but notice that this alligator only had one good eye. Todd then told me to tape his legs together. When I was finished the poor gator looked more like an oven-ready chicken in Tesco's than a frightening killer. My final task was to carry the gator the hundred yards from the pool-side to the truck. Todd lifted the gator up and stuck him under my left arm for all the world like a large handbag, albeit one which could bite my arm off if it set its mind to the task. Compared to Bart the python he was light as a feather and I had time to smile at a few of the locals as I raced out to the truck. Despite the alligator's relatively small stature, the fact that he was completely bound up, and the fact that I didn't seem too worried about him, I noticed that everyone still stood well back. In Miami there can never be such a thing as a friendly alligator.

And so ended my career as an exotic animal collector. I was still in one piece and had learned a fair amount about the strange wildlife which inhabited this sub-tropical part of the United States. I had also seen a few animals. It was time to put away my catchpole and get back to civilisation.

7

Five Million Dollars Modest

Real Estate

*T*he city of Miami has had a short but eventful history involving wars, hurricanes, refugees and crime but without doubt the single most momentous occasion in the 150 years of its existence happened on the evening of 16th September 1984. That date marked the television début of a show called *Miami Vice* and from then on the city would never be the same. The potent combination of large-fitting jackets with permanent two-day stubble and a selection of stunning Art Deco buildings was enough to convince the viewing world that Miami was hip and that the city's chequered past of crime and disorder, which had meant that nobody with any sense went there, should be promptly forgotten. Detectives Crockett and Tubbs may go down in law enforcement history as the only police officers who lived in yachts, drove Ferrari Testarossas, wore only Armani, and never shaved but they certainly succeeded in creating a shiny new perception of Miami as a place of never-ending sun and style where even the baddies had cheekbones to die for. Dying, by the way, was something only done in slow motion with a rock backing track.

Before *Miami Vice* helped trigger a new future the city had been seen as a place where the baddies, many of whom had no cheekbones and some of whom were not very good-looking at all, were winning. The early Eighties in Miami were dominated by crime, drugs and racial tension and even the thought of an average temperature of 75 degrees from that permanent sub-tropical sun was no longer enough to entice people to visit. However bad things got the city never stopped being the first and only port of call for hundreds of thousands of Latin Americans who dreamed of enjoying the Yankee lifestyle and flooded into the area from Castro's Cuba and other Central and South American countries. Then Don Johnson did some smouldering from behind his Ray-Bans and the whole world, not just the Latins, wanted to live in a Deco place off South Beach. The Miami property boom had begun and the only tension in the streets now was amongst decorators worrying that they were going to run out of pink paint. My final job assignation in America was my chance to surf Miami's success wave and cash in on that boom. I had been taken on as a real estate salesperson. Who was I kidding? I could give the job any fancy title I liked but it would not hide the truth. I was about to clock on as an estate agent.

The company I was to work for was a local firm called Wimbish-Riteway Realtors. When I saw the spelling of the name Riteway I thought it had the ring of British trade names like Kwik-Save or Kwik-Fit so I readied myself to sell discount houses at knock-down prices while wearing a blue boiler suit. I soon discovered that company names are not always everything they seem. Wimbish-Riteway turned out to be state of the art realtors working at the very top of the premier league of American estate agents and dealing only in prices which sounded more like lottery wins than house values. I was told that back in 1993 Carlos Justo, one of the partners in the company, had won the title of Number One Residential Real Estate Person in the World because he had sold $70 million worth of property in that single year. Seventy million dollars is a lot of houses; that's Birmingham plus change. I wonder how many fibs about being a stone's throw from the shops he had to tell to earn that kind of money?

So, I was to be an estate agent, a much maligned job back in Britain although I personally had nothing against members of the profession. Except for that awful greasy man in Tooting, and that woman with the bad teeth in Birmingham. In America real estate personnel were actually valued members of the community and once they made it to the Carlos Justo level they could probably become President if they felt like it. I wasn't sure exactly what skills would be expected of me in the job but I did work out that image was probably fairly important so I got up at the crack of dawn to prepare myself and my face for the day ahead. Up until that point my Miami jobs had not demanded the highest standards of dress and make-up. At least I'd heard no complaints from the alligator or any criminal about my fashion sense and 'practical' had been very much my watchword when I was dressing for the beat and the wild animal trail. However, now I was going to attempt to sell multi-millionaires multi-million dollar houses so it seemed to me that the very least I could try and look was a million dollars. When the taxi arrived to pick me up at eight o'clock I really did feel that sum and a few dollars more in my long beige Armani jacket, dark skirt and high shoes. When you look good you feel good and I felt I was in impressive shape that bright Miami morning. If an Eskimo had come anywhere near me at that moment he would have ended up owning a time share in an igloo. I was hot.

The driver at the wheel of the huge yellow estate cab was a bear of a man and when he turned round to check the address I was almost blinded as the morning sun reflected off the bullion on his teeth. His name was Joseph and he was from Haiti, another troubled Caribbean country which had transported huge numbers of its people to Miami. He was a man of few words but began to talk a little about the problems Haitians faced back home and as he spoke I noticed that his face was marked with some vicious-looking scars. Joseph had paid some terrible price in his life but I didn't feel that I knew him quite well enough to enquire about the details. Instead I concentrated on watching the scenery as we drove towards Indian Creek Island where Carolyn Miller, the senior partner of Wimbish-Riteway, lived. Indian Creek Island is part of the slim finger of Miami Beach which looks like a giant natural breakwater between the city and the Atlantic Ocean. Joseph took us north through Miami on the main US 95 expressway, then turned east and drove out of the mainland city on the Broad Causeway across Biscayne Bay to Miami Beach. I have to say that I expected to find a bit more over there than a succession of dull, regimented rows of houses and motels and as we headed west through the area evocatively known as Surfside I became totally unimpressed. If I had wanted to visit a boring seaside town I'm sure I could have found one back home *and* it would have had a decent cup of tea available at all times, unlike here.

Then suddenly the cab left the arid wastes of City Bungalow and the windscreen filled with stunning Mediterranean images of sun-bleached stone and shady palm trees. We crossed over a sparkling narrow waterway on a picturesque white bridge and stopped at an immaculate gatehouse. We had landed on Indian Creek Island. I had to announce myself and my reason for visiting to the man at the gate and I couldn't help but notice that he was a bit more imposing than just another security man. He was actually a real Miami Police Department policeperson, just as I had been such a short time ago.

Indian Creek Island might have been less than a square mile in size with only around thirty houses and an exclusive golf club to take care of but the powers that be had decreed it merited its own official police force. Money, I was discovering, talked loudly in this part of the world and on Indian Creek it shouted. The officer looked at me and Joseph suspiciously until I mentioned Carolyn Miller's name. Then he virtually touched his forelock, or to be more precise, touched where his forelock would have been if there wasn't a police hat jammed down a millimetre from his eyebrows. He waved us through and called me Ma'am.

We cruised slowly along a wide road with an immaculate golf course straight out of a magazine on one side and a series of huge houses in large landscaped grounds on the other. Some of the houses did look impressive but the overwhelming sense I got was of Weybridge with palm trees although, to be frank, it was really Surrey without the sparkle because there was a lifeless quality to the whole place. I'm no golfer but I've always believed that a golf course looks better with people playing on it. This course was so perfect I swear you would have had to search hard to find a single blade of grass out of alignment. Unfortunately, in order to achieve that state it seemed they had banned that annoying habit people have on golf courses of wanting to hit a white ball with sticks. There was not a pair of lime-green trousers nor a diamond-patterned cardy in sight, which I suppose was a mercy in a way.

Carolyn lived at number 23 and the ordinariness of the address made it sound like just another house to me. We pulled into her drive and I discovered then that it was far from that. I had left Weybridge behind and entered Scarlett O'Hara country. The house was an impressive mix of Southern Colonial and Ancient Greek styles with just a dash of Barratts. I could see a central fountain dwarfed by columns of giant palms and a pillared entrance guarded by two stone lions. I'd swear it was blooming Tara and the astonishing realisation crossed my mind that the owner was only the estate agent. What would the clients' properties look like?

Carolyn Miller greeted me on the steps of her residence and it was clear that she matched the place exactly. She was tall, elegant, very expensively dressed and it was quite impossible to tell what age she might be. Her house turned out to be no more than seven years old so I would guess Carolyn was somewhat the senior of the two. She seemed genuinely excited that I was to join the company and suggested we get to work right away. We strolled to one of the four garages around the main drive and Carolyn picked out a vehicle to complement her navy blue outfit. I'm just guessing that was the basis of her choice but it would certainly have made sense. When you have gone to the kind of money and trouble she had to look the way she did, it would be just crazy to ruin the effect by climbing into the wrong car. Her elegance ruled out the BMW Z3 sports car, because it is so hard to enter gracefully, the yellow Rolls-Royce clashed terribly with her gold jewellery, and the Lexus was simply a bit *arriviste*. Today it just had to be the black Bentley which gleamed with a kind of showroom perfection as Carolyn opened the door and invited me to sink into the air-conditioned soft-leathered splendour of Old England on wheels. It goes without saying that Carolyn Miller was a very rich businesswoman who happened to be married to a very rich businessman. To them recession was something that happened to men's hairlines before expensive transplant surgery rectified the problem. She had been working in real estate for over twenty years and had certainly cornered the Indian Creek market. In the last decade there had been fourteen sales amongst the thirty-odd houses there and she had been involved in thirteen of them. The rogue sale was a deal struck between two residents who cut out Carolyn by agreeing every-thing privately between themselves. I imagine she could just about bear the loss of commission. In between the chirping of her mobile and bizarre conversations with her office she told me about her sales techniques which she described as being 'very soft'. I asked if any of the phone calls which had interrupted my training were about multi-million dollar deals. She gave me a faint smile and said, 'All of them.' Silly me. Carolyn revealed that she sometimes needed to spend over two years selling a property to a particular client. With prices around the $8 million mark and commission at 6 per cent it seemed to me that it could still work out profitably if she took twenty years to clinch the deal.

Carolyn had decided to take me to a property on the island about half a mile or so away from her place so that I could get the feel for the kind of house I would be attempting to offload later. This house was owned by the Moss family and was on the market for $8.9 million. I suppose they were trying the old '99p' system in that price tag. $8.9 million sounds so much cheaper than $9 million, don't you think? The house looked very unspectacular from the drive but I got a shock when Carolyn threw open the double doors to reveal a huge and airy space beyond. I felt the way Doctor Who must have done when he had his first test drive in the Tardis. She quickly swept me through to the back of the house to bask in the stunning view of Biscayne Bay which shimmered through a glass wall of floor to ceiling windows. It was not the number of bedrooms or bathrooms, or whether it was a stone's throw from the bus stop which was the critical selling point of this house, it was the view. That vista of Biscayne Bay was what clients would really be buying because when you have the kind of silly money needed to compete in this market you could easily afford to change every other detail. The décor, the furniture, the structure of the house itself, all could be transformed at a price but the location would always look the same, hurricanes permitting, of course. Carolyn took me on a tour through the Tardis, stopping to admire the downstairs cloakroom with gold fittings and the second-level living area which had the eerily untouched air of a showhouse. In the master bedroom at the end of the house was a gigantic bed which looked as if it had never been ruffled by human contact so I set down my dignity on the bedside table and took a flying leap onto the counterpane. Carolyn laughed in a faintly embarrassed way and suggested that perhaps spontaneity could be the key to my selling style but perhaps not quite such spontaneous spontaneity.

The bathroom in this house was perfect. Perfect, that is, if you planned to take your ablutions while accompanied by the entire playing staff of the Miami Dolphins football team. Everything was on the grand scale here but nothing was really to my taste. Carolyn told me that I should just try to sell the features which I liked, as well as having facts about the state of the market in the area up my sleeve, and armed with that I should be able to sell anything to anyone. I had watched her closely since we met and I noticed that she said everything in a calm and quietly proud voice which never showed much in the way of emotion. That all changed when we got to the closet off the master bedroom. Carolyn was suddenly so moved that I am sure I saw one of her hairs go out of place. She called it a closet, but I would liken it more to a John Lewis storeroom. All I could see were row after meticulous row of clothes and shoes covering all the walls. I listened as Carolyn waxed lyrical about the value of a closet like this to potential buyers. A symptom of wealth is obviously the need to put all your shoes in neat lines and as I admired the extensive selection of slippers I kept getting an image of a certain Philippine dictator's wife and her footwear hobby. Nobody needs quite as many shoes as Mrs Marcos collected but it looked as if whoever owned this house was going to have a good old go at matching her. Why would anybody *want* a closet this size? I have always found that the back of the chair in my bedroom is the ideal place for me to arrange my wardrobe. It's not quite as organised but it works for me.

Carolyn then took a call on the mobile from her partner Carlos, the incredible super-salesman I had been told about, who was going to drop by. He meant this literally as I discovered when I heard the roar of a descending helicopter arriving in the back garden. We watched the grey and white helicopter gently touch down on the back lawn and saw a yellow blur speed towards us. Before I knew what was happening I had been grabbed by the arm and dragged into the helicopter. I was at 150 feet in the clear South Florida air before I caught my breath and realised I was now in a strange chopper with a strange man who had his arm round me. Carlos Justo was a deeply tanned, shaven-headed ball of real estate energy wearing a vivid yellow shirt with a kind of royal crest, white trousers, no socks and expensive loafers. The helicopter engine screamed above us but I had no trouble hearing what he was saying to me mainly because he was shouting it precisely one inch from my right ear. Carolyn had just given me a taste of soft selling, now I was at the other end of the sales spectrum.

Carlos liked to take prospective clients up in the helicopter because it gave them more of the most precious commodity in their busy lives, time. He could show them the whole of the Miami area in fifteen minutes against the five hours it would take him by road. We flew around Indian Creek Island and I got the chance to see why people would pay millions of dollars to get a place there. It looked like a millionaire's paradise with its line of huge properties in two-acre plots of land ranged along the coast and the manicured expanse of the golf course backing onto them. Julio Iglesias must have sold a lot of records because he could afford to build himself a stunning Polynesian-style house along the road from Carolyn. It was either Polynesian or from Dorset because Julio's place appeared to have a thatched roof. As we cruised through the cloudless sky Carlos explained to me more about the art of shifting fantastically expensive houses. First you had to find your clients, people who could lay their hands on the required amounts of cash and this being America nobody seemed to mind exactly how they had come by that cash. Carlos talked with pride about dealing with royalty, Mafia, Presidents and drug dealers and revealed that a new wave of clients was coming from Russia and Hong Kong. These people shared one common bond and it came in folding form with Presidents' faces on it.

We flew down the thin stretch of Miami Beach passing La Gorce Island where Cher has her Tuscan palace, then over the Art Deco splendour of South Beach which was now the hippest location in the whole of America. The area has become the symbol of the renaissance of Miami over the last fifteen years as its faded glory was gradually restored and enhanced by developers and, importantly, by the gay community who colonised the area before it became fashionable again. Now it was to die for, darling. Carlos pointed out the tiny oval of Star Island which was aptly named because several of them lived there including Hispanic Miami's greatest export, Gloria Estafan. She has two houses on the island but don't think of that as a sign of Estafan greed because one of the two is not for living in, it's just for having parties. That's all right, then.

Star Island looked a lot more cramped than Indian Creek because Carlos informed me that houses were built in one-acre plots rather than the two acres which was the rule on Indian Creek. We continued flying west along the length of the concrete arrow of Macarthur Causeway which linked the tip of South Beach to the mainland, and headed over Brickell Avenue where many of the plots are even less generous at half an acre. I found it hard to believe people would spend huge sums of money to live bang up against their neighbours but over here that did not seem to be a consideration. Maybe they have local rules about how loud they can play their stereos. Brickell had always been considered a bit downmarket until Sylvester Stallone did a neat bit of business. He bought a massive eleven-acre plot for $8 million and built an enormous mansion. Just along from his spread the Material Girl herself, Madonna, has also bought a place. They must have seen her coming, if you'll pardon the expression, because she only managed to get one acre for five million of her dollars. The house she had built there was a kind of Mediterranean red-roofed, two-storey job which looked quite modest to me. Carlos laughed and said, 'Five million modest . . .'

The helicopter headed north following the line of Bayshore Drive which looked strangely familiar to me despite the fact I had only been to Miami briefly once before. Then I realised the pilot was in fact re-enacting the opening sequence of *Miami Vice* which lovingly detailed the concrete and glass towers which forest that stretch of coastline. Was that a hint of designer stubble I could see on Carlos? Yes there was, but unfortunately it was on his shiny scalp rather than his chin. He informed me that the time had come for me to learn to be a real real estate saleswoman and he was taking me back to Indian Creek where I could look around a property he was about to pitch to clients. I would have the chance to see it, then briefly practise my selling skills before he did it for real. It was not just any property we were flying towards, this was the former residence of no less than the sister of the Shah of Iran and it was on the market for a staggering $7.9 million. By the way, for that sum you would get precisely three bedrooms. A snip. As we landed in the back garden all I could see was a grey concrete sprawl set in an open grassy plot and my heart began to sink. I ran with Carlos towards the house and as we approached the back entrance I had the terrible realisation that the architect's main influence for this building had been the Smethwick Sports Centre, circa 1966. The price tag may have been spectacular but the property certainly wasn't. The tropical sun burned fiercely, the bay glittered, the lush turf shone impossibly green but this house sat colourless, squat and misshapen bringing an unwelcome echo of Sixties British civic architecture to South Florida. I hated the place already and I hadn't even set foot inside the door yet. Carlos was oblivious to my inner turmoil as he dragged me into the echoing expanse of the main 'Grand Space' and asked me excitedly what I thought. Luckily the question was rhetorical, as were all his questions, and he had turned away before I could mutter my response. 'It's unbelievable,' I whispered.

A sprawling, contemporary waterfront masterpiece, perfectly integrating design with luxurious surroundings was what I should have been thinking because that was what it said about this house in the Wimbish-Riteway brochure. Sprawling I could accept but none of the other words applied, as far as I was concerned. The huge reception area was a gigantic forty feet by fifty feet marble-floored space with a sixteen-foot ceiling. It looked like the Ibiza Airport Departure Lounge but without the welcoming feeling. The room was completely empty except for one piece of furniture which had been left by the previous owner. A gold sofa, which told me all I needed to know about whoever he or she was. He was, in fact, a Greek property speculator who had bought the place from the Shah's sister twenty years ago, left it untouched, then four years ago had it completely remodelled. *This* was remodelling? The house was a mass of conflicting styles and really did look as if it had been designed by a committee. Not an architectural one, more like the Smethwick Scouts Under-Twelve Football Selection Committee. The horror just never stopped as I moved from room to bizarre room. The downstairs bathroom was incredible and must surely have been an elaborate joke on the part of the designer. It was completely covered in tiny inch-square mirror tiles which made a trip to the loo more like being trapped on some sick-making white-knuckle fairground ride. Just as a punchline the actual bathroom mirror in a bathroom of mirrors was too small to be any use. Up the horrendous set of marble stairs things did not get any better. The master bedroom was completely soulless and needed a good shag-pile carpet to make it habitable, and the unspeakable main bathroom looked as if the designer had consulted his book of design styles and decided to use everything. There was one detail of the bathroom which was pretty much perfect. The room had been sited in exactly the right position at the front of the house to make anyone emerging mermaid-like from the sunken bath perfectly obvious to the golfers putting for birdies on the fourteenth green just across the road. Nice touch. By now I was in a state of deep décor shock and I had one piece of advice to impart to any prospective buyer. Knock the place down.

Carlos was on a hot streak. He had just sold $10 million worth of property in the last two days and I was about to witness at first hand just why this remarkable man was so good. Now in his mid-thirties he had come over to Miami from his native Cuba fifteen years ago to make his fortune like so many others before him. Carlos actually succeeded beyond his wildest dreams by focusing his great energy and force of personality on the world of real estate and by 1993 he was the number one salesman in the world with that extraordinary $70 million year. The young man from communist Cuba then got a swift lesson in the downside of capitalism and promptly lost his fortune when he made a misguided move into the construction business. Carlos had to trade his $6 million house for an apartment and start all over again. Now he was enjoying a second wave of success but the profits would have to go to pay the taxes on his initial success which the US Government was currently pursuing him for. Still, Carlos seemed quite happy about everything, considering. I found myself doing the 6 per cent commission sum in my head on all these amazing deals of his but Carlos was at pains to point out that money he made also had to be split between a large back-up team. He then introduced me to Robert Evangelista, one of his assistants, who was a handsome, and I think the word is flamboyant, New Yorker. I discovered that when Bob was not playing on the Carlos team he was indulging his passion for ballroom dancing which took him to Blackpool every year to watch the World Championships. I found it very hard to visualise the fragrant Bob sashaying down the Golden Mile but apparently he never missed a trip to the Miami of Lancashire.

Carlos wanted me to practise my selling skills by pitching the place to Bob. I took a deep breath, looked around the Grand Space and suggested to Bob that he should hire the demolishers, then build a proper house. I thought Carlos was going to have a coronary as he screamed my name and told me to stop. What I had just said was no less than real estate sacrilege. No wonder his face showed genuine pain. I apologised but I was only being true to myself and there was a limit to how far I would go in this job. Acting may be my real trade but to play someone who liked this house would have required the performance of a lifetime. Carlos then proceeded to give one. His clients were a very tall South American businessman and his tiny wife who had been looking in the area for six months or so. They arrived in a giant stretch limousine and it was instantly obvious from their eloquent body language as they looked around that they hated the house. It was time for Carlos to go to work and after fifteen minutes of non-stop real estate poetry their mood had completely changed. 'I know you don't think this is the place for you,' he smiled at the impassive sunglassed face of Señor South American Businessman, 'but this is a house which is perfect to fulfil your dreams.' I noticed that he paid special attention to the lady as he tried to convince her that this was the ideal place to entertain. Whether it was what he said, the way he said it, or some magic powers of voodoo, a quarter of an hour later Carlos had his arm around the Señor, was smoking one of the Señor's big cigars, and was discussing sorting out a contract with him which would take the place off the market for a month. Not only had Carlos almost sold the house for $7.9 million but he had also convinced his clients they needed the empty two-acre plot right next to it for another $3.5 million. I found it hard to believe what I was hearing but I now knew for sure that I was in the presence of true real estate greatness. I have to admit that I felt inspired as I left Indian Creek Island after Carlos's display but no amount of sales brilliance from my mentor would convince me that house was not a dump. Señor Businessman was welcome to it.

And now it was my turn. The next day Carolyn called me to say that she had found the perfect property for me to sell. Apparently it was brand new to the market and 'an amazingly beautiful' house. On current form I decided that I would probably be the judge of that. The amazing thing was that the house was even better than she described it. Casa Baja had been built three years ago in one of the best locations in the whole of Miami, out in the Coral Gables area of the city, and it sat at the tip of a headland between Biscayne Bay and the Gables Waterway. There was so much water around this house that being there felt more like sailing in an ocean liner. But what a liner. The house was a Mediterranean pink and white picture and the interior was the most tasteful I had seen since arriving in Miami. Why anyone would want to sell it was a mystery to me until I discovered that the couple who lived there were in the process of divorcing and this sale was the inevitable and sad result. Real estate people don't like to talk about it but although divorce and bankruptcy may be terrible for civilians, they make great business for them. One divorce can trigger a whole series of property deals and it's jackpot time at Wimbish-Riteway. First the family house goes, then the split couple need new individual homes. Carlos also quietly suggested to me that there is sometimes another deal included which is often the most difficult of them all to complete. A new place for the mistress, apparently. It was heart-breaking to see signs of the happy family life which had obviously once filled this house. At the barbecue area near the pool I saw a display of casts of the smiling faces of all the family beaming down at me. Then I realised that a real real estate person feels no emotion and so I shrugged my immaculately attired shoulders and went to work.

Casa Baja was listed at $8.9 million and, for once, I thought that seemed like a fair price. It is amazing how quickly one can get used to talking about millions if one sets one's mind to it. The house had just gone on the market and the clients I would be selling to were the very first people to see it. I wondered to myself if people impulse buy at the $8.9 million level. Carolyn gave me the detailed specifications which looked a bit Greek so I decided to concentrate on the key facts. The house had been built in 1994 in the 'Tropical Mediterranean' style by a firm of noted local architects, there were five bedrooms, eight full bathrooms, and all the living space was on the first-floor level except for the office in the tower at the top of the house. All the rest of the information would be patter. Sell the location, the view, the weather, the lifestyle, had been the advice from both Carolyn and Carlos. I didn't need to memorise air-conditioning system details to do that. I also had a genuine belief in the quality of the house which would help my performance and I had a trick up my Armani sleeve. Carolyn told me that the master bedroom furniture had been hand-built in Bath which gave me an excellent bit of personalised selling information. Surely with a fact like that delivered in my accent, no respectable person of the American persuasion could remain unmoved. I was on a winner. Now, what was 6 per cent of $8.9 million?

Another good omen came in the shape of my clients' car which was a black top of the range Jaguar. They obviously liked British things and they were about to experience a British saleswoman so the odds were probably stacked even higher in my favour. Ed Archer was a late forties business type with one of those flat-top haircuts beloved by the Americans. He was something very senior in an airline and was relocating to South Florida with his family. His wife was called Birdie and that was exactly what she was like. They seemed charming and, more importantly, very keen to find a house to suit them. Apparently they were torn between Miami and Boca Raton, a rich man's enclave on the coast north of Miami which they preferred because the security was better, but they looked as if they might fall for, I mean listen to, my spiel. Everything went perfectly until we were in the master bedroom. I had shown them the fabulous view and let the beauty of the location do my work for me and they were definitely impressed. Especially when I pointed out that the furniture had been made in Bath, England. They were pretty much eating out of my hand at that stage and I was sure that they would have signed the contract right there if I had produced it. Then Ed fixed me with his steely gaze and asked how much of the property was 'under air'. I had not the faintest idea what he was talking about. I was about to take a guess when he translated for me. It meant how much of the place was air-conditioned. I did not have a single clue – my revision had not been good enough. For a second I flashed back to being at school and the awful feeling I used to get when I looked at an exam paper and realised it was too late to do the swotting. Ed then started talking about his interest in boats and I could feel a technical question steaming towards me. Sure enough, moments later he was asking if his forty-five-foot sailboat which drew five feet could be moored at the house pier. I had a clearer idea about whether there was life on Mars than the answer to that one. Ed was polite as I stammered an improvised answer but I sensed that he was less than impressed. However, he and Birdie still seemed interested and while we were in the kitchen she actually said that she could 'envision us here, dear'. I got a swift envision of the commission cheque at that point. Ed then asked about the possibility of buying the house lock, stock and barrel and I heard myself talk about preparing a contract for that kind of offer. They asked to have a look around on their own and I took the opportunity to call Carolyn in the office to check the answers to the list of questions I had not been able to answer. There was still a chance.

I took the Archers out to the front of the house to give the final twist to their wealthy arms. We strolled past the pool to the croquet lawn which they got excited about, especially when I said I could throw in the hoops for nothing, and then headed for the small stretch of sand on the Waterway side of the property to watch the setting sun. It was now nearly six o'clock and the evening sun was like a giant tangerine on the horizon as we stopped on the strip of man-made beach to watch it slip into the ocean. I gave the Archers the last blast of the Carlos treatment with lots of stuff about dreams and fulfilment, then put in some of my more practical advice. I reminded them they were absolutely the first people to see this incredible property and with the Dow Jones at an all-time high this was the time to buy before prices sky-rocketed.

Then Ed ruined the moment totally. For some reason he wanted to know where the sand had come from to make the beach we were standing on. I suppose I went onto a kind of autopilot and I heard myself in the distance saying the word,

'Arabia.' A piece of advice here. In America the use of irony is prohibited in many states and needs a licence in the others. Florida was irony-free and Ed Archer was not impressed by my answer. I think my hopes died at that second. I could guess what was going through his mind. If a salesperson could tell such a bad fib, then he or she did not really deserve to be trusted in anything else they said. The Archers didn't say much more but got back into their car and politely told me they had a lot of thinking to do. In my heart I knew the truth and, frankly, I didn't really care. I felt absolutely drained and all I wanted to do was go home and go to bed. Before I got there, though, I had to go through another Carlos experience as he analysed my performance blow by blow. He told me I had done a good job and despite my dumbness on important details the Archers were genuinely interested. I noticed Carlos's arm was around me in very much the same way as it had been wrapped around Señor Businessman. I was being sold a line.

The next day was my last as a Wimbish-Riteway operative and Carlos decided I should face the ultimate challenge. Selling the sister of the Shah of Iran's house to Terence Conran, perhaps? Careful with that irony again! No, this time I had to take another super-rich couple to Star Island to sell them the house of their dreams. There was just one teensy weensy little detail to take into consideration. The house did not exist. I was actually selling a one-acre plot of scrubland which was on the market at $4 million and having to use a fantasy sales pitch to make it sound desirable. I gave it my best shot and the couple loved my imaginary house so much they decided to buy it. Unfortunately, their imaginations were so developed that they imagined the house could be on another site and decided against shelling out the several million dollars for my Star Island plot of land. The

Archers lost interest in Casa Baja and, as far as I know, that house remains unsold.

Carlos and Carolyn were complimentary and grateful to me nevertheless and paid me the $200 wage cheque due to an inexperienced assistant salesperson. That sum would of course be topped up with my share of commission for the successful deals I was involved in. Actually, $200 can go a long way, if you make a real effort. My days at the real estate coal face were over and I was glad, even though Carolyn genuinely offered me a job with her company. She felt that I would be a success because people believed me but I wasn't sure if I believed her. I admired the ambition and achievement of Carlos and Carolyn but their unreal world filled with unreal money and unreal people was not for me.

The next day I got back in my flying saucer and returned to the galaxy far away that I called home. My American voyage was over and as I began re-entry to normality over Heathrow I had time to consider the lessons of my trip. I realised it would be wrong of me to use my New York and Miami experiences to generalise about the whole of the United States because those two cities are very distinctive parts of the extraordinary fusion which makes up America. However, earning an honest buck in them gives at least a taste of the American Way of Work. Toiling alongside the inhabitants of Planet America in those two great cities taught me that what I was doing was work, but not as we know it. The Americans probably have a higher work ethic than we British usually demonstrate, certainly take fewer holidays than us, and enjoy a freedom from the restrictions of class which allows even the lowliest job to be celebrated as worthwhile. They believe in a competitive team spirit in their places of work which can harness extra effort from individuals and they do like to have a nice uniform for many of their jobs. They live in a Can Do world where nothing is a problem for long and good service comes naturally but, sadly, they ruin all these splendid qualities by not having one person around who knows how to make a decent cup of tea. This was one Alien who was hanging up her spacesuit.